MW00967176

10/26/2009

Lateral Approach **to** Managing **Projects**

Simple principles for achieving high customer satisfaction and mutual profitability

Ho Wing Sit
And
Ling Bundgaard

Published by Lateral Approach Publishing
www.LateralApproach.com

Library of Congress Control #
2009904519 (TP) ; 2009904525 (HD)

Publisher's Cataloging-In-Publication Data
(Prepared by The Donohue Group, Inc.)

Sit, Ho Wing.
   Lateral approach to managing projects : simple principles for achieving high customer satisfaction and mutual profitability / Ho Wing Sit and Ling Bundgaard.

   p. ; cm. -- (Lateral approach)

   ISBN: 978-0-9824689-1-3 (TP)
   ISBN: 978-0-9824689-6-8 (HC)

1. Project management. 2. Executive ability. 3. Consumer satisfaction. I. Bundgaard, Ling. II. Title.

HD69.P75 S58 2009
658.404   2009904525

658.405
Version 9-15-09

Value, not clearly identified, will be
discounted or not recognized at all.

When it comes to creating value, no detail is
unnecessary.

- Ho Wing Sit

I dedicate this book to my loving wife, Ingrid, and my children Christopher and Nicholas. For my children, I believe you will find treasures at every crossroad and detour throughout your life journey.

Ho Wing Sit

ACKNOWLEDGEMENTS

Nothing quite moved me to work on this book series as did my sons, Christopher and Nicholas. My wife, Ingrid, gave me the strength, luxury, and perseverance to pursue my belief. I couldn't have come this far without my co-author, Ling Bundgaard, who has long shared her breadth and depth of knowledge from working with the biggest companies around the world. I gratefully acknowledge former Lt. Governor of California, Leo T. McCarthy, former Governor of Hawaii, George R. Ariyoshi, and the many executives, mentors and "mystics" I have encountered over the years. They inspired me to embrace their values and share their wisdom. They are the ones who contributed the gems in the Lateral Approach series. My sincere thanks to Deborah Papp, my editor, who helped fine-tuned the messages while enabling me creative freedom. My special acknowledgement to my designer, Sukanya Sarkar, who helped bring the books to life through color and graphic expression.

Introduction

Many books have been written on project management techniques. *Lateral Approach to Managing Projects* presents a new perspective on implementing projects aimed at achieving high customer satisfaction and mutual profitability. Projects are becoming increasingly more complex, and, historically, complex projects have a higher statistical probability of failure. You will learn from this book new insight for creating successful projects. You will learn new approaches to meeting contractual obligations and overcoming problems caused by ambiguous terms. You will learn new disciplines for creating and increasing the value of your services and deliverables. You will learn how to overcome hurdles and speed up customer acceptance even when conditions are less than ideal.

Lateral Approach to Managing Projects also introduces structured rapid implementation methodology with four powerful exercises: Exercise to Create Your Own Success; Exercise to Empower Your Client; Exercise to Assert Your Authority; and Exercise to Carrying Out Your Leadership Role.

In a short story format, we present to you a great deal of what we have learned from our corporate Mystics and proven experiences. We recognize the importance of these distilled experiences. We also recognize that the people, who work with you, whether as managers or as peers, may someday look to you as one of their sources of wisdom.

Read this story with the intention to immediately share your discovery with your peers and managers. With the mindset of sharing, practice what you learn immediately. These powerful principles and concepts apply equally to corporate and non- corporate environments.

You are reading this book because you want to know more. We hope that we enrich you with new perspectives or reinforce something you might already know.

Table of Contents

Chapter 1- Failed Project

It was not a good morning for John. A client phone call had catapulted his company into damage control mode. He summoned one of his project managers, Scott, to his office.

"I asked you to come over because I just got an earful from Johnson's Pharmaceutical. They basically want us to stop work. They believe our system stinks. They feel that we don't know what we are doing. They even asked me to compensate them for project delays. This is one very unhappy customer.

"Plus, I just heard from Accounting about our own cost overrun. We are going to lose our shirt on this project, not to mention our reputation. I want to hear what you are going to do about it." John looked hard at Scott and waited impatiently for an answer.

A dead silence filled the room for what seemed an eternity. Scott had never seen John in this mode before. He had hoped that it would not come to this although he had known the project was going south for some time now. Nervously, Scott answered.

"I don't know what to say. I am not doing anything differently at Johnson's Pharmaceutical than with other projects. Our product has been proven in the field. It worked at other sites and it worked at Johnson's as well. We just have a very difficult customer." Scott knew it was a bleak defense even as he uttered it.

John was becoming even more upset as Scott answered. "Look, Johnson's is paying several million dollars more than other clients. Of course they expect more and expect to be treated differently. What I am hearing is that they are not happy with what we're giving them. Johnson's may very well be a tough customer. What they perceive is their reality. You have to deal with it and correct this situation. And Scott, you need to review your performance at other projects also. They aren't great either."

"Yes sir," Scott quietly acknowledged, lowering his head.

"I am very upset with you, Scott. You should have brought the Johnson's situation to my attention much sooner and emphasized the importance and urgency.

"Scott, you are very smart and able. You have a future in this company. I still believe in you. So I used all my pull and credibility to strike a deal with Johnson's Pharmaceutical to basically restart the project."

John tempered his reprimand with some encouragement. "But it would not be right for me to just send you back to the Johnson's project until you can convince me that you can do better. Here's what will help you. I want you to pay a good friend of mine a visit. Afterwards, get back to me so I can make a decision. I want you to get back to me quickly," he instructed.

John quickly scribbled something on a yellow sticky note and handed it to Scott.

Scott was very apologetic and at the same time thankful that he had not lost his job. Nervously, he accepted the note, saying, "I am sorry for what happened. I will do my best to correct this situation and thank you for considering giving me another chance."

John signaled Scott to leave. Feeling disappointed with himself, Scott took a look at the yellow sticky note. Written on it was:

Call the Mystic at 283-9888

Scott was a little puzzled. Who was this Mystic? What could he do for him in this predicament? He told himself not to speculate and quickly followed up on John's instruction.

To Scott's surprise, the Mystic was willing to meet him that same afternoon. When Scott walked into the Mystic's office, the receptionist seemed to be expecting him.

"You must be Scott. Our Mystic is waiting for you." The receptionist was cheerful and rose to escort Scott into the Mystic's office.

"Yes, I am Scott. By the way, how should I address him?"

"Well, everyone who came here for advice eventually started to refer to him as the Mystic. That title stuck. Now we all call him that. It is OK for you to do the same," the receptionist happily explained as she ushered him through the Mystic's door.

The Mystic extended his hand to Scott as he entered. "Scott, I was expecting you. John just called and explained the situation to me. It is a difficult situation, isn't it?"

Scott was a little caught off guard by how quickly and succinctly the Mystic had arrived at the subject at hand. "Uh, yes, it is a difficult and embarrassing situation," he acknowledged.

"John asked me to give you some guidance to help you turn this project around. I don't know what I can do. What do you think?" the Mystic probed.

"Yes, John gave me your number," Scott said, trying to catch up.

"Well, what do you think I can do for you?" the Mystic repeated.

"I don't know what you can do about a tough customer," Scott replied, telling the Mystic what he felt was at the root of the problem.

"So you think it is the customer?" The Mystic listened empathetically as he reflected on Scott's answer.

"The product didn't help either," Scott added.

"You think the product is also part of the problem." The Mystic continued to listen and reflect.

Scott was becoming a little defensive. "I tried everything and I have implemented a lot of systems successfully in the past."

"That's good. You think you have tried everything already." The Mystic gave Scott a little encouragement.

"Yes!" Scott responded emphatically.

"Tell me, Scott, what did you really try to do at Johnson's?" the Mystic asked, encouraging Scott to think deeper.

"Come on, you know what implementation and project management is about." Scott wondered why the Mystic was asking such an obvious question, and felt a little insulted. "We install and set up systems and get people trained to use the system. For me as a project manager, I see to it nothing gets dropped, that we deliver our system on time and on budget."

"That sounds simple enough, doesn't it? the Mystic said. " But how do you achieve a high degree of customer satisfaction? How do you make projects profitable for both sides? That takes a little more, doesn't it?"

"When it comes to customer satisfaction, the customer is king. We do what customers want us to do." Scott quoted what he believed to be a universal truth.

"What about profitability?" the Mystic challenged.

"We charge accordingly." Scott gave his standard answer.

"Well, if you just charge your client regardless, won't that sort of kill your client's budget? Is that good business? Or if your company eats the costs, won't it kill your budget? Is that good business?" The Mystic raised even more thought provoking issues.

"I didn't think about it that way." Scott was caught off guard by the questions. He found he didn't know the right answers.

"You mentioned Johnson's being a tough client. All companies have to deal with customers of all kinds. Some may be more difficult than others, like Johnson's. Wouldn't it be beneficial to your career to have the knowledge and experience to handle customers of all kinds, under all kinds of situations?"

What the Mystic said seemed quite compelling to Scott. He took the bait as his enthusiasm to know more increased.

"Of course it would be good to have that knowledge and experience. I am a member of a professional project management institute and read very extensively on the subject already." Scott was proud of his professional training background and questioned whether the Mystic could add substantially to what he already knew.

"That is excellent. That means you have the basic foundation for doing a good job. I hope I can help you think laterally, extending from what you have already mastered, and boost your project management skills from good to great. Do you think you want that? Can you handle it?"

"Of course!" Scott answered confidently and with pride.

The Mystic nodded. "Listen then, our time is short. You have a crisis on your hands. You don't have weeks to learn. You have hours and at the most a couple of days. Then you will have to execute in the field. We have to utilize our time well."

Scott began to sense the urgency. His heart began to race. He liked the tempo. It felt like the pace of rapid implementation.

"I am with you all the way, Scott confirmed. "Tell me what you want me to do."

"Let us start by discussing the role of leader and how leadership applies to project managers. Not having a clear idea of your own role is a common pitfall. It can doom a project from the start."

The Mystic paused to let Scott think about what he had said, then added," I am sorry, I need to excuse myself for fifteen minutes. Let's talk about this some more when I return. OK with you?"

"OK," Scott agreed with some reluctance. He was a little confused, saying to himself, "Leadership, management, what's the difference? What does it have to do with dooming a project? We get in. We get the job done. We get out. That's that."

But as Scott dug a little deeper, he acknowledged that almost all projects turned out to be not so straightforward. It seemed like they always ended up getting stuck, dragging on, and at the end required compromises on both sides just to get through it. Not that every client was unhappy. On the other hand, most were not exactly cheering either. Projects that came in on time and on budget were, in fact, few and far between.

Before long, the Mystic returned.

"Sorry for the interruption. Have you given what I said some thought?" he asked.

"Yes, and I am a little confused. In the past, I have always thought of myself as a pretty good project manager. I am focused and I don't let things drop. I may even be a little aggressive in pushing projects to meet schedule." Scott tried to be humble, but he thought of himself as being more than just pretty good. He thought of himself as one of the best in his profession.

"I believe you are a good manager. Are you a good leader?" the Mystic challenged.

Scott was somewhat surprised by that question. "What does leadership have to do with project management? We have our statement of work, and our job is to get the work done. Isn't that enough?" Scott frowned as he gave his answer. It seemed so straightforward to him.

"Well, there is a little bit more to it than that." The Mystic smiled at Scott.

"What would that be?" Scott asked.

"Let's take a step back, to before a project starts," the Mystic said, trying to help Scott think through the sequence of client interactions. "What would your company be doing with your client then?"

"That would be before the deal was closed and the contract signed. We would be selling our client on our products and services," Scott answered, puzzled.

"What happens during the sales process?" the Mystic continued.

"We demonstrate our products and explain our services to help the client make the decision to select us as his vendor."

"So, what happens after a client selects your company?"

"We sign a contract and mobilize to start implementing the project," Scott answered.

"That is what happens at your company before a project begins. What do you think happens on the client side?" the Mystic continued.

"I am not sure." Scott was lost. He wasn't sure where the Mystic was leading him.

"Well, your client's company commits itself, its employees' professional reputations, and sometimes their careers to your company, products, and services.

"At your company, you might celebrate winning the project. But your client might be losing sleep and getting nervous. The reliance and dependency on you to successfully guide them through troubled waters and onto the Promised Land creates a situation and a need for leadership. Am I making sense?" The Mystic was careful to paint a picture from both the client's and the vendor's perspectives to illustrate the obvious need for leadership in such a situation.

"I have never thought of it from that perspective," Scott admitted, "Now I can see where leadership may play a role."

"As a matter of fact, do you know that your clients often value leadership more than even your products and services?" the Mystic asked.

"You must be kidding me. How can that be? Weren't our products the deciding factor?" Scott challenged.

"Yes, products play an important part in the decision process. But there is more to it. Have you not heard of companies paying a premium for brand name consulting companies to implement third party products?" the Mystic challenged back in a cool and steady manner.

"I always wondered about that," Scott smiled.

"Indeed, your client is paying your company a lot of money for your leadership. Your client looks to you to show them the way to break new ground and rise to a higher level. You can be sure that if your clients knew how to lead the charge themselves, they wouldn't be hiring your company in the first place.

"To deliver value and earn your keep, your job must be to embrace the leadership role, shoulder the responsibility, and properly utilize the authority that comes with being a leader." The Mystic spoke with conviction and definitiveness. His experience in this matter came through strongly.

Scott recognized that the Mystic had made a very significant statement. But he was not yet sure what the implications were.

"Now that you have convinced me that being a project manager is more about leadership than about management, what am I supposed to do to create happy customers and successful projects?" Scott asked.

"There are three keys to creating happy customers and successful projects. Once you have mastered them, you will find that project implementation will go more smoothly. Let me write them down for you."

The Mystic wrote down on a yellow sticky note the following:

> **Creating happy clients and successful projects is about:**
> - **Meeting Contractual Obligations**
> - **Creating Value**
> - **Obtaining Acceptance**

Scott took a quick look and felt quite unsatisfied. "Is that it? Aren't you over-simplifying it quite a lot?"

"Not really. That is all there is to it." The Mystic opened his arms wide as he smiled at Scott.

Before Scott could protest, the Mystic continued.

"I know that it is difficult for you to believe. After all, when you are in the field, what you face seems much more complicated and every project has its own demands. Before we talk about what I wrote down, why don't you sleep on it? Let's get together again early in the morning. What do you say?" The Mystic cleared his schedule to meet with Scott the next day.

That night, Scott continued to find it difficult to accept the simplicity of what the Mystic considered to be the keys to creating customer satisfaction and successful projects. As Scott went through in his mind the first of the three keys, he felt that the Mystic was just restating the obvious.

"Meeting contractual obligations," Scott read out loud to himself. "Of course that would make clients happy. I certainly have been meeting our obligations. I certainly have dotted the 'i's' and crossed the 't's', yet still I haven't always made my clients happy."
"Creating value." Scott read the second key out loud. "What does that have to do with project management? Delivering the products creates the value. Isn't that enough?" Scott shook his head as he moved on to the third key.

"Obtaining acceptance. Well, wasn't that also obvious? We all know that getting project sign-off is important. How to get there on time and on budget is the challenge, isn't it?"

Scott felt triumphant that he could poke holes in the Mystic's three keys. He felt he knew better. However, his satisfaction didn't last long. After all, he had a problem project on his hands and was not quite sure how to turn it around. What he really felt was exhausted.

Scott reflected on his conversation with the Mystic. He entered into his notebook the following:

Leadership

- To achieve high customer satisfaction and successful projects, it is not enough just to focus, not let things drop, or be aggressive in pushing projects to meet schedule.
- Client Company committed itself, professional reputations, and employees' careers to your company's products and services. Your client's reliance and dependency on you to successfully guide them though troubled waters and on to the Promised Land created a situation and a need for leadership.
- Products and services play an important part in the decision process. Your clients often value leadership more than even your products and services.
- You can be confident that if your client knew how to lead the charge, they wouldn't be hiring your company in the first place. To deliver your value and earn your keep, your job is to embrace the leadership role, carry the responsibility, and properly utilize the authority that comes with being a leader.

- Three keys to creating happy customers and successful projects:
    - **Meet Contractual Obligations**
    - **Create Value**
    - **Obtain Acceptance**

Chapter 2 – Project Management Made Simple

Scott arrived back at the Mystic's office the following morning.

"Good morning, Scott. Did you rest well? Are you ready for more mental breakthroughs?" The Mystic gave out a little laugh.

"Good morning. I stayed up thinking about what you wrote down. The three keys seem obvious and I have to agree that they are important. However, I couldn't get past the obvious." Scott frowned a little as he expressed his frustration.

"That's a good start. You agree with the three keys. Sounds like you want to know more. Do you?"

"That's correct," Scott responded quickly.

"So, what do you want to know?" asked the Mystic, giving Scott the opportunity he wanted.

"To start with, why are there only three keys? I agree that they are important but, in any project, there are many, many milestones and many, many issues. Reaching each milestone and overcoming each hurdle is equally as important as the next. From this viewpoint, I don't understand."

"You are right on the mark. It can be quite confusing, can't it? So many targets, so much to do, and each seems to be just as important as the next. Let us think laterally. Don't you think it would help if only three things really mattered among all the milestones and hurdles?" The Mystic tried to lead Scott to think beyond the obvious.

"Sure. But is that realistic?" Scott asked.

"Why not?"

"Well, it might be true for some special projects. Our products involve hundreds of set-up steps and thousands of services tasks that we agreed to install and perform. Any misstep means we won't fulfill our obligation, we won't get paid, and we'll have unhappy clients on our hands." Scott stubbornly tried to justify his point.

"Aah! What you are saying is that you have many obligations. By not meeting any one of these obligations, your project will fail. Your customers will not be happy. Is that so?" the Mystic continued with patience.

"That's right."
"Well, one of the three keys is Obtaining Acceptance. You must not be confused by the hundreds or thousands of tasks required to get there.

"Your focus is on obtaining acceptance, whatever that may be. If your client is willing to sign off on your deliverables and accept that your job is complete, nothing else matters, does it? And if they are not happy, you will not get sign-off, will you?"

"Well, that's true, but a happy client does not mean acceptance. Meeting contractual obligations means acceptance, doesn't it?" Scott asked.

"I agree with you that chances are you cannot get acceptance without meeting your obligations. More importantly, your so-called obligations, whether they be contractual or verbal, are not as concrete as you may think." The Mystic looked hard at Scott as he led him to think laterally.

"Yes and no." Scott responded as the Mystic expected.

"What do you mean?" The Mystic deliberately put on a puzzled look.

"The client seems to always want more, to interpret contract terms differently, or make changes from what was written in the contract. They hold out on acceptance, I stay firm, and client relations takes a hit," Scott explained.

"In that case, what are your obligations? What does Meeting Contractual Obligations mean?" The Mystic challenged.

"That is straightforward: it means whatever is written in the contract or agreed upon," Scott answered.

"Is that so? Contractual obligations may not be so concrete." The Mystic reiterated what he had alluded to earlier.

"Now I am confused. I thought one of the three keys is Meeting Contractual Obligations. Now you are suggesting that the obligations are not concrete. How can it be not concrete if there is a contract?" Scott frowned, trying to catch on.

"The fact of the matter is, most contractual obligations are grey." the Mystic explained patiently.

"What? How can that be?"

"It can be!" the Mystic assured Scott.

"So, the lawyers didn't do their job?"

The Mystic tried to help Scott to view the situation at a higher level. "The lawyers did their best, but that is all they could do."

"Then, what really happened?" Scott asked.

"Let's try to dig deeper into the purchasing process. What do your clients normally do?" The Mystic again began to lead Scott on visualizing the process.

"They try to compare our products with our competitors. They try to 'kick the tires'. There are times we go through a formal purchasing process by responding to a formal requests for proposals. Our replies are also formal and sometimes binding. In addition, we do the normal selling routine with product demonstrations and brochures. Our clients normally ask many questions. We answer either in writing or verbally. We provide our clients references, etc.," Scott responded confidently.

"So, your clients are doing everything they can to understand and compare your products with those offered by your competitors. What do you think your sales people are doing during this process?" the Mystic continued.

"They are trying to win the clients and get the order as quickly as they can," Scott explained.

"How do they do that? What do your sales people do to win the clients and get the order as quickly as they can? "

"They do it by putting their best foot forward, by 'wowing' our clients with our products and by showing off what we can do better than our competitors," Scott continued.

"That's right! Your company wins because your sales people are convincing," the Mystic summarized.

"Our sales people are good," Scott said with pride.

"When your sales people win and get the order, what do you think the expectations of your clients are?" the Mystic asked, preparing to make his point.

"Oh, their expectations are pretty high." Scott paused a little as he started to catch up to the points the Mystic was leading him toward.

"That's what I expected. How much do you think your clients really know about your products and services when they make the purchasing decisions?" The Mystic was trying to make another point.

"When they make the purchasing decision, they feel that they know enough about the products and services. It does not mean they really know all the detail about our products and services." Scott spoke slower as he began to realize what he was saying.

"How about on your side? How much do you think your sales people really know about your clients' needs?" The Mystic was leading Scott to visualize the process from a 360 degree angle.

"Our sales people normally try to understand our clients' needs. They are very good up to the point of identifying our clients' hot buttons. That is probably the depth they need to make the sale. They probably do not go much beyond that," Scott answered truthfully and realistically.

"How about people who will be managing the project? Don't they get involved during the sales process?" the Mystic continued.

"Yes. At that stage, it is not as if we are providing consulting services. We ask questions that might give us some insight into the complexity of the engagement. We try to understand the details of our clients' needs, still at a high level. On the other hand, we also are busy telling our side of the story; telling our clients how great we are and putting our best foot forward." As Scott explained, he began to realize and appreciate the enormous complexity and lack of clarity among the different perspectives and roles.

"Am I hearing that all the parties have a general understanding of each other's needs? Do you think your clients, your sales people, or your own project people know enough to translate all that information into detailed contractual terms?" Finally, the Mystic delivered his punch line.

"That would be very difficult, if not impossible. There is never enough time to go into the kind of detail needed until projects begin. There are risks on both sides. On the other hand, both sides think there are enough details in the contract to protect them. Chances are both sides are merely seeing what we want to see, and hearing what we want to hear." As Scott responded, he realized that he had answered his own question to its fullest extent.

The Mystic leaned back in his chair and emphasized the point he wanted to make. "You are so right. The end result is problems with expectations and assumptions."

"That is, indeed, what we constantly have to deal with in managing projects," Scott admitted.

The Mystic brought his point to a final conclusion. "So, what can the lawyers do to provide more clarity to this situation?"

"Not much, especially from a boilerplate contract," Scott agreed.

"From this respect, I wasn't far off saying that contracts are almost always grey, am I? The mutual expectations may be far apart. This is the source of unhappy clients and vendors." The Mystic smiled, satisfied that he was making a believer out of Scott.

"Now I see where you are coming from," Scott responded, but added with concern, "Then how do we meet contractual obligations?"

"That's what we need to talk about." The Mystic gave Scott another smile, knowing that he was about to help Scott overcome a mental block and see the root causes of project problems.

He stood up, signaling for Scott to follow him.

Scott reflected on his conversation with the Mystic. He entered into his notebook the following:

Project Management Made Simple

- Project implementation can be quite confusing due to the many targets, to-do's, etc., and each seems to be just as important as the next. The Lateral Approach points out only three things that really matter – **meeting contractual obligations, creating value, and obtaining acceptance.**

- On meeting contractual obligations, client seems to always want more, interprets contract terms differently, or makes changes from what was written in the contract. Client holds out on acceptance and vendor stays firm. Client-Vendor relations take a hit.

- If you don't have a happy client, you will not get sign-off.

- Most contractual obligations are grey.

- In the purchasing process, clients make purchasing decisions thinking they know enough about the products and services. It does not mean they really know all the product and service details.

- In the selling process, sales people normally try to understand the clients' needs and clients' hot buttons. That is probably the depth the sales people need to make the sale. They probably will not go much beyond that.

- In the selling process, consulting services people ask questions that might just give them some insight into the complexity of the engagement. They may try to understand the details of clients' needs, but probably still at a high level.

- In the selling and purchasing process, both client and vendor think there are enough details in the contract to protect them. Chances are both sides are merely seeing what they want to see, and hearing what they want to hear.

- Contracts are almost always grey. Mutual expectations may be far apart. This is the source of unhappy clients and vendors.

Chapter 3 – Key # 1 - Meeting Contractual Obligations

"Need any cream in your coffee?" the Mystic asked Scott.

"Please. Coffee is just what I need." The break was putting Scott a little more at ease.

"Is this discussion helping you?" the Mystic asked, checking progress.

"It was confusing at first. I have never spent the time thinking through the issues that you brought up," Scott confessed.

"You see, if you don't know what your contractual obligations are, you really can't meet them, can you? If you can't meet your obligations, you cannot get acceptance, can you?" Casually, the Mystic tried to help Scott think laterally.

Scott looked up at the Mystic. He was hooked. His curiosity had gotten the best of him. "When you put it this way, the challenge becomes visible. What can be done about this situation?"

"This is where Lateral Approach management can be effective. It is really quite easy. Start by accepting the fact that contractual obligations are grey." The Mystic pressed his points.

"How would acknowledging and accepting that contractual obligations are grey make a significant difference?" Scott wanted to know.

The Mystic did not answer Scott right away. He walked up to the white board and wrote:

**Satisfying contractual obligations
is a matter of getting the client to
accept the deliverables
and
use the product for business**

The Mystic went on to explain. "The first part of the statement is telling you that the products and services may vary from the letter of the contract and still fulfill the contract if the client is willing to accept your products and services. By signing off on acceptance, your client implicitly waives or substitutes items which may be in the contract. This makes the process of gaining acceptance extremely important."

"Now I get it. When the contractual obligations are grey, what really matters most is the client accepting the deliverables. obtaining acceptance becomes the key instead, doesn't it?" Scott wanted to confirm.

"You are getting it," the Mystic encouraged.

"What is the second part of the statement saying about using the product for business? Isn't acceptance and sign-off enough?" Scott asked, a little puzzled.

"The second part of the statement is telling you that, while acceptance is extremely important, it isn't enough to meet contractual obligations nor is it as final as you might have thought."

"What else must be done to satisfy the contractual obligation?" Scott asked.

"The fact that your client accepted the products or services and officially signed-off, by itself, does not mean that you have satisfied the full extent of the contract. The product must also be able to perform as originally intended – to conduct business. By having the client use the product, you generate tangible financial benefits.

"It is the expectation of what the product can or cannot do that commonly generates client dissatisfaction or causes them to hold you to your obligations," the Mystic answered with intensity and emphasis.

"But, I thought the client waived all that through his acceptance?" Scott was puzzled again.

The Mystic used a corollary to simplify his explanation. "Think about it this way. You bought something from a store. You paid for it and you took the merchandise home. You might even have tried the product out. The acceptance process occurred. Still you might return the merchandise for one reason or another, right?"

"That happens." Scott seemed to be catching on.

"My point is, acceptance by itself is not enough to ensure that your customer is happy and that he will not return the merchandise," the Mystic explained.

"Then what will ensure it?" Scott asked.

"The customer has to use the product at a minimum and preferably over a period of time," the Mystic explained further.

"Why do merchants regularly accept returns?" Scott asked.

"Well, they do it to make happy customers," the Mystic explained patiently.

"Happy customer aside, how would using our product make meeting contractual obligations final?" Scott was puzzled again.

"When your client uses your product to do business, he is, in fact, getting financial benefits from your product. And if your client uses the product over a period of time, costing you money while he derives financial benefits, he will have a difficult time justifying non-acceptance. You are in a position to insist that he cannot justify it because it is not equitable." The Mystic answered Scott's question with some very practical business logic.

"What does that mean exactly?" Scott asked.

"It means either your client should accept your deliverables or stop using your product. You do have the right to ask your client to stop using your product if he does not accept delivery, you know."

"I can see the leverage. What will happen if I obtain acceptance from a client and later he decides to stop using the product? " Scott asked from a different perspective.

"Technically, you may believe that you have satisfied the contract. Think about this. After your client spends a lot of money on your product, maybe millions of dollars, and he cannot use it to do business, do you expect him to just write it off? Or think he might go after you, even to the extent of suing you?"

"Our client may not prevail in a lawsuit," Scott challenged.

"You will never know if your client will prevail until the court or arbitrator decides. Do you really want to find out?" the Mystic challenged back.

"Boy, it isn't very clear-cut!" Grimly, Scott realized the complexity and the issues involved with meeting contractual obligations. It wasn't as clear-cut as he had thought before this conversation with the Mystic. Before, it seemed as if, by working hard, focusing, and checking off the contractual details, he could safely assume that he would meet contractual obligations. Now, he wasn't so sure.

"Precisely," said the Mystic, "it isn't as clear-cut as we would all like. On the other hand, you will be all right if you distinguish courtesies from obligations."

"What's that mean?" Scott responded as the Mystic expected.

"Throughout your project implementation process, you will constantly be challenged to balance providing products and services according to contractual obligations, and to extend beyond the contractual products and services as a courtesy. It is a balancing act." Carefully and slowly, the Mystic began to lead Scott to another example of lateral thinking.

"What is your advice on achieving this balancing act?" Scott asked.

"Putting it humorously, count the bullets you fire like Clint Eastwood does in the movies. Each time you deliver a courtesy, count it and hold your clients to a courtesy in return, even to the extent of buying you a free lunch." Both Scott and the Mystic gave a little laugh.

"Why? I would think my client would expect me to be buying lunch." Scott was thinking about the 'client is king' principle.

"Not in this case. It is very important to train your clients to pay and to feel obligated, because it reverses the role. Instead of your client doing you a favor by using your system, the reverse role positions your clients to owe you for improving their work and business," said the Mystic seriously.

"I think I am beginning to like this Lateral Approach stuff. That's very interesting!" Scott laughed.

"Good! What this really means is that while your contract may be grey, your objectives and priorities are no longer grey. With clarity of objectives and priorities you will approach the project differently. You will refocus on finding ways not only to make your client accept your deliverables, you will find ways to enable him to use your deliverables sooner rather than later. You will focus on finding ways for your client to derive financial benefit by doing business with your products."

The Mystic looked at Scott and challenged him to think laterally. "Can you think of something that you will do differently now?" he asked.

Scott was excited now. "Oh yes. If I think of meeting contractual obligations as being black and white, I would tend to think of our work as a lump and my delivery like more of a big bang. Using the Lateral Approach that suggests that handling contract obligations are, in fact, grey, I would certainly break down our work into smaller chunks. This would make acceptance and use easier."

"Very good. Can you think of anything else?"

"Well, if I were to report to our client that my work was 80% complete, he would have difficulties accepting an incomplete job. If I were to break down my work into 100 discrete tasks, I would report to my client that 80 tasks were completed and 20 more were in progress. I can see that my client would have no reason not to accept the 80 completed tasks and might possibly pay for the completed work sooner," Scott answered enthusiastically.

"You've got it, Scott," the Mystic replied. "That is the power of the Lateral Approach. Do you think it will make a difference in the Johnson's Pharmaceutical project?"

"Oh yes, indeed!" Scott continued to feel the excitement. He wondered why it hadn't dawned on him before how this seemingly simple idea could be so powerful. He began to see many possibilities.

"Are you ready for more Lateral Approach thinking?" the Mystic asked, knowing that Scott was now ready and willing.

"Yes, yes." Scott was eager to hear more.

"Have you heard the joke about this very special computer expert?" The Mystic was having fun.

Scott reflected on his conversation with the Mystic. He entered into his notebook the following:

Meeting Contractual Obligations

- Lateral Approach management begins by accepting the fact that contractual obligations are grey.

- Satisfying contractual obligations is a matter of getting the client to **accept the deliverables** and **use the product for business.**

- Deliverables may vary from the letter of the contract and still fulfill the contract if the client is willing to accept your products and services.

- When the contractual obligations are grey, what really matters most is the client accepting the deliverables.

- While acceptance is extremely important, it isn't enough to meet contractual obligations, and acceptance is not as final as most people might think.

- The fact that your client accepts the product and officially signs off, by itself, does not mean that you have satisfied to the full extent contract delivery. The product must also be able to perform as originally intended. At the minimum, it must allow the client to use the product to conduct business.

- If your client uses the product over a period of time, he will have a difficult time justifying non-acceptance that costs you money while he derives financial benefits. You do have the right to ask your client to stop using your product if he does not accept delivery. That gives you leverage.

- Throughout a project, you will constantly be challenged to balance between providing products and services according to the contract versus extending extra products and services as a courtesy. This is a balancing act.

- In the course of balancing favors and obligations, you must count favors and hold your clients to favors in return.

- Training your client to feel obligated is very important because it reverses the role. Instead of your client doing you a favor by using your system, the reverse role positions your clients to owe you for improving their work and business.

- While your contract may be grey, using lateral thinking, your objectives and priorities are no longer grey.

- With clarity of objectives and priorities you will find ways not only to make your clients accept your deliverables, you will find ways to enable them to use your deliverables sooner rather than later. You will find ways for your clients to derive financial benefit by doing business with your products and services.

Chapter 4 – Key #2 - Creating Value

Scott was pleasantly surprised that the Mystic wanted to tell a joke. It was certainly a welcome break. He could not help but laugh as the Mystic took on the demeanor of a computer nerd and repairman.

"This international company's central computer system was down, impacting their operation worldwide. Every minute the system was down, the company was losing millions. Ted the IT Manager tried and tried to fix the system, but couldn't. So Ted called in Josh, a very talented computer expert, for help. Within 30 minutes Josh arrived in his T-shirt and sandals. Josh connected his laptop to the system. With a few key strokes, the system problem was resolved and company operations were back to normal.

"Everyone was happy until they saw Josh's bill. Talk about sticker shock: Josh's bill was for $50,000! Ted didn't know how to explain to his boss how just a few minutes of work could cost so much. So Ted confronted Josh. 'Josh, you were here for less than 15 minutes. How can you charge me for $50,000?'

Josh smiled as he pointed to his bill and answered, 'Well, $100 is for the time I spent. $49,900 is for the key strokes.'" Scott laughed as the Mystic delivered the punch line.

"Well, what do you think? Is Josh over-charging?" the Mystic asked.

"He socked it to Ted, didn't he?" Scott answered.

"That reaction is almost universal. It may be funny, but did Josh over-charge Ted?" the Mystic asked again.

"It certainly comes across that way to me," Scott answered, sensing it was not the answer the Mystic was waiting to hear.

"But what Josh did probably saved Ted's company millions. Have you thought about that?" The Mystic asked, prompting Scott to think laterally.

"It seems like such an easy fix, though," Scott said, trying to justify his answer.

"If it was so easy, why didn't Ted do it himself?" the Mystic challenged.

"Probably, after Josh did it, Ted felt stupid. Ted probably felt that he could have or should have been able to fix it himself."

The Mystic smiled as he nodded in agreement. He had heard what he wanted to hear.

"We can debate whether it was easy or whether Ted could have done it himself. The crux of the problem stems from the fact that Ted didn't think he had gotten his money's worth. Josh's value and contribution didn't come across," the Mystic explained.

"But Ted is a smart guy. Why couldn't he relate to the value and contribution you are talking about?" Scott was somewhat puzzled by the Mystic's answer.

The Mystic pointed his finger to his own head and said, "Sometimes value is measurable in the form of equipment, monetary savings, training, time, etc. Often, value is created in the mind of the client; in the form of expectations."

"What do you mean?" Scott asked.

"The lesson here is that you can generally assume that value not clearly identified will be discounted or not recognized at all. When it comes to creating value, no detail is unnecessary. You have to point out every one," the Mystic emphasized.

Scott didn't get it. "What makes you think that?" he asked.

"That is just human nature. People only see what they expect to see and hear what they expect to hear," the Mystic explained patiently.

"Am I hearing you say that, had Josh spent the time to point out to Ted beforehand or afterwards that he would be paying a premium for his service, and that the premium was worth it and well deserved, then Ted would have been more ready to accept a large bill?" Scott tried to interpret what the Mystic was saying.

"Yes. Had Josh made the effort to create value, Key #2 to creating satisfied clients, then Ted would have felt that the $50,000 bill was a bargain." The Mystic confirmed Scott's understanding.

Scott's face lit up. "Why doesn't everybody do that?" he asked.

The Mystic answered matter-of-factly, knowing well that most people don't follow this Lateral Approach.

"Think back how often you have not done that because you assumed your value and contributions were obvious to other people. Not everybody thinks laterally."

"Hmm, that might explain many things." Scott looked up at the ceiling while he remembered such examples.

"Let me give you another example," the Mystic said. "It is actually more a paradox than just an example. If a consultant takes 1,000 people hours to complete a job at $200 per hour, he deserves to charge $200,000. If a second consultant only spends one hour to do same job, what should he charge?

"Should it be $200 for his one hour of work, $200,000 for getting the same amount of work done, or a premium at perhaps $300,000 since he did it faster?" The Mystic seemed to be having fun posing the question.

"Let see," Scott answered hesitantly. "I would like to say $200 but then the second consultant seems to be substantially under pricing his services at that amount. $200,000 seems fair because the first and the second consultant did the same amount of work. But then the second consultant seems to be over-charging. Then again, the client benefited from getting results sooner, which should be worth more."

"As you see, it doesn't make sense for the second consultant to charge only $200. If so, why work fast? Why not drag the work out and charge more? Where is the incentive? Right?" the Mystic challenged.

"Right," Scott concurred, albeit a little hesitantly.

"How would you feel if the second consultant were to charge $300,000 instead of $200?" the Mystic continued.

"Wow, I would feel that the second consultant was way over-charging for his services," Scott admitted.

"But he wasn't over-charging at all," the Mystic happily argued. "It is precisely the opposite situation. By completing the job early, the second consultant may have saved his client millions of dollars, and that equates to a lot more value than what the first consultant provided.

"After all, the client can enjoy the benefit of the deliverables 999 hours sooner. Just imagine the cost savings and the financial benefits. Certainly, a case can be made that the $300,000 charged by the second consultant was more than fair."

"I see the lateral thinking," Scott finally agreed.

"This is what I am talking about. Unless the second consultant points out the benefits and value to his client, like most people, he would feel exactly like you: that he was over charging." The Mystic made his point.

"This thing about benefit and value is good to know, but how would it apply to my case?" Scott asked.

"Chances are you and your people on this project have not been pointing out the benefits and value of the many, many products and services you are providing to Johnson's Pharmaceutical." The Mystic took on a more serious look again.

"What do you mean?"

"Let me point to another example. There was a time when getting an oil change for your car cost less than $20. Probably there are still oil change services available for that price. Then came Jiffy Lube's 18 point 'Signature Services' oil change. Jiffy Lube advertised their services as being fast. In-and-out was what you could expect. Think about the win-win scenario. Faster service now meant added value, and high efficiency meant improvements to the corporate bottom-line.

"Taking it one step further, chances are you could not walk out of the place for less than $50 what with add-on sales, and yet the customers kept on coming back. Why?" Once again, the Mystic was leading Scott toward lateral thinking.

"Why?" Scott still wasn't sure how this related to him.

The Mystic was happy to clarify his point. "Jiffy Lube built a company around the concept that value, not clearly identified, would be discounted or not recognized at all. As such, Jiffy Lube services create value by pointing out in plain English and on a big sign the 18 point signature service they will perform for you. You can trust their services. But can you imagine: one of the 18 points is visual inspection of wiper blades. Another one is visual inspection of exterior lights. These services have little value unless they are packaged together and pointed out. As such, value is being created just by pointing out seemingly trivial things."

Finally, Scott caught on and could relate the principle the Mystic was sharing with him to his current project.

"Now I am seeing the possibilities," he exclaimed. "I can imagine all the things we have done that are totally hidden from the view of our clients. Johnson's Pharmaceutical surely has taken many of our deliverables and courtesy work for granted. When we are on-site, our client can see what we are doing. But when we work off-site, our client has no feel or appreciation for what we have to go through for them."

"You're getting it. To create value, take a closer look at your statement of work. Take the trouble to explain and educate your clients about what you are doing. These are important steps to creating value," the Mystic instructed.

"That, my team and I can do." The excitement was building up. Scott's mind was teeming with ideas.

"What about the example we talked about earlier, like breaking up a large task into 100 discrete tasks? Are we creating value by doing that?" the Mystic probed, checking to see if Scott truly understood the principle.

"Oh, yes, I can see it now. That is another way to make our work easier to understand and be appreciated. I can charge for partial payment and obtain milestone acceptance easier," Scott responded happily.

The Mystic agreed, making sure to directly relate lateral thinking and the principle of creating value to project management. "Isn't getting paid and obtaining acceptance what project management is all about?" he asked.

"What about project status reports? I can visualize status reports as a tool to communicate and create value," Scott said.

"That's right! Now that you understand the principle of creating value, your reports should reflect that principle."

Scott was very excited as he thought of more ideas and possibilities. "What about an on-the-job training program? I can get more client participation, and my client can get more practice. I can see that this is a win-win approach. I can see that it turns a favor for our client into a billable effort."

"Oh yes!" the Mystic encouraged.

"What about showcasing the application or system for my clients? I can treat the interaction as a demo or I can treat the interaction as preliminary training. As a demo, my clients would treat the interaction as a favor to me for watching me sell them something. As preliminary training, they would owe me time and material."

"Oh yes!" the Mystic encouraged further.

"What about controlling expectations? I can create value in the mind of my clients by keeping expectations realistic. If I set my clients' expectations too high I will be setting myself up for a fall. I can also see that if the benefits are not immediate, I need to control expectations by focusing on longer term and future benefits from the start. Meanwhile, I still need to deliver value. So, I must make sure my clients recognize the specific areas in the products and services that are producing value." Scott was seeing all the different possibilities from different perspectives.

"Oh yes!" the Mystic agreed again.

"In summary, everything my team and I do should be communicated and translated into value and benefits for my clients. They should feel that they are getting more than their money's worth.

"Now I can really appreciate the importance of creating value as a key to managing projects for high customer satisfaction and mutual profitability," Scott reiterated, eager to apply these newly learned principles to his failed project.

He continued. "Thanks. It isn't as if I didn't know the importance of creating value. It is just that I have not consciously done it or done it consistently. Neither has my team. You have just awakened me to this important aspect of successful project management." Scott spoke sincerely and reached out to shake the Mystic's hand.

"I am glad that this conversation has helped. Do you know that practicing creating value will lead you to obtaining acceptance?" The Mystic felt that Scott was ready to move on to the next important area for turning his failed project around.

The Mystic paused to take a sip of his coffee. He stole a glance at Scott.

Scott's mind was spinning with possibilities. He regretted that he had missed so many opportunities before that had resulted in his clients at Johnson's Pharmaceutical feeling unsatisfied. Now he also saw the way to win his client back.

Scott reflected on his conversation with the Mystic. He entered into his notebook the following:

Creating Value

- Sometimes value is measurable in the form of equipment, monetary savings, training, time, etc. Often, value is created in the mind of the client in the form of expectations.

- You can generally assume that value, not clearly identified, will be discounted or not recognized at all.

- When it comes to creating value, no detail is unnecessary. You have to point every one out.

- It is human nature for people to only see what they expect to see and hear what they expect to hear.

- We often mistakenly assume that our value and contributions are obvious to other people.

- Imagine all the things that have been done that are totally hidden from the view of clients. Clients surely have taken many deliverables and courtesy work for granted.

- Take the trouble to explain and educate clients about what you are doing. These are important steps to creating value.

- You can create value by breaking up large tasks into smaller discrete tasks. Deliverables in smaller chunks are easier for clients to understand and appreciate.

- Status reporting is a tool to communicate and create value.
- On-the-job-training is another way to create value.
- There should be no more product demos after a sale closes. As a demo, your clients treat the interaction as a favor for watching you sell them something. As preliminary training, they owe you time and material.
- Everything your team and you do should be communicated and translated into value and benefits for your clients. Your clients should feel that they are getting more than their money's worth.
- You can create value in the mind of your clients by keeping expectations realistic. If you set your clients' expectations too high you will be setting yourself up for a fall.
- If the benefits are not immediate, you need to control expectations by focusing on longer term and future benefits from the start. Meanwhile, you still need to deliver value. Make sure your clients recognize the specific areas within products and services that are producing value.

Chapter 5 – Key #3 - Obtaining Acceptance

The Mystic took a look at the clock. He nodded with satisfaction at Scott's progress. After all, Scott was an experienced project manager. All he really wanted to do was to help Scott break new ground by thinking laterally.

"Scott, can we cover Key #3 before we break for lunch?" The Mystic was gauging his time.

"I'm with you," Scott nodded in agreement.

"In that case, tell me your perspective on obtaining acceptance."

"Well, I gain acceptance by focusing on dotting the 'i's' and crossing the 't's'," Scott answered matter-of-factly.

"How do you dot 'i's' and cross 't's' when the contract is grey as we concluded earlier?" the Mystic challenged.

"I don't know what else to do. That's the hurdle we face. Often my client and I don't agree and that's

73

how projects drag on and our profit margins get killed." Scott was uncertain as he answered the Mystic's question.

"Isn't that the truth!" the Mystic exclaimed in agreement.

"Well, what is your perspective on obtaining acceptance?" Scott challenged the Mystic.

"Acceptance is more about confidence, deployment, and reaching agreements to move forward. It shouldn't be confrontational," the Mystic stated.

"But the client that holds up acceptance usually points to differences in the interpretation of deliverables, product features, and other details like that. The client points to the missing dot on the 'i' and the cross on the 't'," Scott answered defensively.

"When your client went through the exercise to dot 'i's' and cross 't's' with you, he was, in fact, telling you that he did not have confidence in you, that he was not ready to deploy, and that he was not in agreement with you to move forward," the Mystic answered back definitively.

Scott continued to be defensive. "If we did our part, why shouldn't the client give us acceptance?"

"When the contract is grey, as we concluded, how would you or your client know what your parts are?" the Mystic challenged.

"So, how would you handle such a situation?"

Plainly and firmly, the Mystic answered. "Reaching agreement to move forward is a key to obtaining acceptance."

"How do you do that?" Scott asked.

"Reaching an agreement to move forward with your client implies willingness to trade off, look ahead, become practical, or adjust expectations," the Mystic explained.

"So what does that mean for me?" Scott questioned.

"It means you must educate and maneuver until your client comes to the realization that he can derive more benefits by moving ahead than by standing still and insisting on something he might or might not get." Once again, the Mystic was helping Scott to think laterally.

"What are some of these benefits that I can point out to my client?" Scott asked, still not quite getting it.

"The benefits for your client of moving forward with you can be in the form of prestige, recognition, political gains, cost savings, not having to obtain more budgets, ability to obtain more budgets, and so on," the Mystic answered.

"I can point out benefits like that. What if we still can't agree?" Scott wasn't so sure.

"That's why deployment plays an important part. You want your system to deploy in part or in whole. You want your client to derive economic benefits as soon as possible. Incremental acceptance and incremental successes are all techniques to deploy in some form or other. It helps your client build confidence in you and in the system." The Mystic was bringing together the principles expressed earlier.

"So, deployment helps gain acceptance?" Scott wanted to confirm.

"Deployment by itself may not be an official sign-off. In a way, deployment allows you to compel acceptance, especially when your client derives economic benefits from your system. When your client begins to derive economic benefits, holding up acceptance become inequitable." The Mystic reiterated the principle expressed previously. Now the importance of the principle in relation to obtaining acceptance became more obvious to Scott.

"So it's kind of like the next best thing," Scott acknowledged.

"Let's say that it is a major vote of confidence," the Mystic replied.

"How do you gain the confidence of the client in order to obtain the final acceptance we want?" Scott pursued.

"Gaining confidence and building trust from your client will not occur overnight. It is built up from the very beginning of the project," the Mystic answered.

"What must I do?" Scott asked again.

The Mystic got up and walked to the white board. He wrote the following:
- **Set and Meet Expectations**
- **Empower Your Client for Flexibility and Change**

"Two things," he replied. "First you set and meet expectations, and second, you empower your client for flexibility and change." The Mystic read what he had written on the white board.

"Setting expectations, I know about that already," Scott said dismissively.

"So, how do you set expectations?" the Mystic challenged.

"I lower my client's expectations," Scott replied.

"I am sorry, Scott; it is a bit more than lowering expectations. Just lowering expectations reduces your value to your client," the Mystic explained.

"Then what is it?" Scott asked.

78

Calmly, the Mystic continued. "It is true that during the selling process clients sometimes tend to hear what they want to hear and see what they want to see. They decide to buy from you because what they think they heard and saw meets their expectations. During implementation you will be challenged to bring your clients back to reality, back down to earth. Resetting expectations, not lowering expectations, is done by focusing on solving the business problems at hand that will create the most value."

"What about the differences in expectations?" Scott asked.

"If you were to follow what I said about focusing on solving the business problems at hand, you would realize that differences in expectations normally result from wanting to use different methods to solve the same problems. Keep in mind, your client has become accustomed to doing business and solving problems in a certain way over many years," the Mystic explained.

"Then how do you overcome history, tradition, or customs?" Scott continued.

"It is not simple for your clients to visualize and adjust their systems and procedures to yours overnight. At the same time, remember that it is your way of doing business that your clients have purchased," said the Mystic.

"You've hit the nail on the head," Scott acknowledged. "That is exactly the source of confrontation."

"Resetting expectations requires you to explain and clarify to your client what they have purchased – in the beginning and not at the end of the project. You need to explain whether your company is selling standard or custom systems. If your client is sold a standard system, you need to explain what constitutes customization. You need to explain upfront that 'doing it your way' is a form of customization and costs extra." The Mystic pointed out a common pitfall.

"How do you do that upfront?"

The Mystic paused. He walked to the white board and wrote:

SAY WHAT YOU DO

80

DO WHAT YOU SAY

The Mystic proceeded to explain. "You can reset and meet expectations and build confidence and trust by following this principle." The Mystic pointed to the white board. "Say what you do and do what you say."

"I thought I always do that," Scott countered.

"Really? Then you shouldn't have an unhappy client at this stage," the Mystic stated.

"Why?"

"Had you executed the first part of the principle, that is, to SAY WHAT YOU DO, and your client disagreed with you, your project would not have proceeded this far, would it?" the Mystic answered.

"That is true. My client would have raised hell in the first place," said Scott, acknowledging that what the Mystic was saying was starting to make sense.

"Precisely. In essence, you want to know upfront if there is any chance of meeting your clients' expectations and making them happy clients. By doing that, neither you nor your clients will be blindsided," the Mystic continued.

"Suppose I do tell my client what I will be doing. Then what?" Scott asked.

"This is the part many people tend to forget, that is, following up with DO WHAT YOU SAY. The two actions, SAY WHAT YOU DO and DO WHAT YOU SAY, must go hand-in-hand. If you think hard about it, if you have to do what you say, you will be clearer and more careful about what you say you will do in the first place. In fact, your first action should be to reach agreement and reset expectations, and the second action should be to deliver against the promise and expectation. If you really follow this principle, you can be confident that you will meet your clients' expectations," the Mystic said with conviction.

It was becoming clearer to Scott at this stage." Now I understand. I think I can do that," he said.

"I am glad you feel you know how to set and meet expectations. However, that is still not enough to gain sufficient confidence from your client to obtain the final acceptance you want," the Mystic said, steering the conversation back to the original subject.

"Why?" Scott asked, a little disappointed.

"It is true that by the time you meet the expectations you set for your clients, they will have begun to have confidence and trust in you. However, that is a far cry from them having confidence to take over the project from you. Your shoes may be hard to fill from your clients' point of view." The Mystic was leading Scott to his second point.

"What would happen then?" Scott asked.

"Your clients would drag their feet. They would try to hang on to you. At the moment you ask for final acceptance, it would become a wake-up call for them that the responsibility for the system will be passed from your hands to theirs. Suddenly, they would feel that they have not learned enough about the system to take on that responsibility. They would not be so confident in themselves. It would become less about you than about them."

"But, we always provide training for our clients," Scott said, feeling a little frustrated. He knew that in working with clients he had followed the implementation methodology, which covered all aspects of training, education, and more. He couldn't understand why his clients wouldn't be able to let go and move forward on their own.

The Mystic tried to help by relating to Scott's own experience. He asked, "Listen, how did you get to where you are today? Did you get several days of training and suddenly become the expert?"

"Of course not!" Scott replied. He was a professional, proud of his own expertise and capabilities. "I became what I am by solving a host of different problems, by using the system over many years. Nowadays, systems are getting to be more complex, with many moving parts."

"Precisely!" the Mystic exclaimed. "In order for you to help your clients help themselves, you must help them build confidence in their own ability to handle the system. You must empower them. You must..." The Mystic pointed to the second bullet point on the white board: **Empower your client for flexibility and change.**

"Yes...." Scott looked thoughtfully at the white board again.
"The best place to start is by communicating your empowerment approach to the senior managers at your client site who have profit and loss responsibilities," the Mystic pointed out.

"Why?" Scott asked.

"You want to convince and obtain cooperation from the top. You want to let management know that by empowering their people and their team, they won't have to run to you every time they encounter a problem." The Mystic began to explain the Lateral Approach to empowerment.

"Why would management want me to do that? Why would I expect their cooperation?"

The Mystic explained, "Simple. Since you charge for your services, empowerment makes sense to anybody who understands the financial impact of having to pay you each time something comes up. Your client surely doesn't want to be on-the-hook for your services or be held hostage by your services. Let your client know that empowerment is an important element of what you deliver at their site. They will understand that it is a win-win approach."

"Well, I am convinced. Now, how exactly am I going to empower my client?" Scott seemed satisfied with the Mystic's answer and was ready to forge ahead.
"As we concluded earlier, you have to have a leadership role. It is your job to inspire your client's team to learn as much as they can about the system you are installing. Pull the client team into your implementation process every step of the way by empowering them to do as much as they can. Remember, each time you do a task instead of having your client's team do that task, you are depriving that team of the opportunity to learn.

"This is thinking very laterally, isn't it?" the Mystic asked.

"It certainly is," Scott answered. "I always thought that it is my team's job to perform all the tasks and to deliver to my client a complete turn-key system. What you are telling me is that I am actually doing my client a disservice instead." The Mystic's words had sparked new insights for Scott. Suddenly, he was breaking through and began to think laterally.

"Many project managers mistakenly think like you do until they learn the Lateral Approach. They don't realize that they are doing their clients a disservice, as well as themselves," the Mystic added.

"Why is it that by doing more for our client it turns into a disservice?"

The Mystic explained the simple logic behind the Lateral Approach. "It really depends on what you are doing more of, isn't it? When you deprive your client the opportunity to learn by doing, it becomes a lose-lose proposition. It requires your company to deploy more resources and, in the end, both your work and the completed system are still a big mystery from your client's perspective. Your client's team feels no ownership and no confidence. Therefore, you've done them a disservice."

"What are you really saying?"

"The empowerment process is a process of transferring ownership and educating your client starting from the beginning of the implementation process until final acceptance," the Mystic summarized. "You want your client's team to be able to say, 'I know the system as much as you and I can take care of it from now on.'

"When your client's team can say that, it means they have the knowledge and confidence to move forward alone. When they can say that, then they will feel comfortable giving you the final acceptance you're asking for."

Scott was hungry to know more. "I can accept that. How do I empower my client's team?" he asked.

"You empower them by allowing them to touch, use, and do as much as they can on the system during the implementation process. You educate, coach, and give them guidelines each step of the way, but you must let them do the work in setting up the system. Let them do their thing. You will be surprised by how much they can do and how far they can go.

"After all, they know their business better than you, just like you know your system better than them. Meanwhile, be generous with your praise and acknowledge their accomplishments." The Mystic gladly shared his experience in leadership and empowerment processes.

"Wouldn't my clients perceive this empowerment approach as our company's excuse for being lazy on our job?"

"That is a good question. A lot depends on how you and your team conduct yourselves and lead the client's team. Instead of behaving like contract labor, you and your team must play the role of coaches and teachers. I have never heard football players complaining about their coach not doing the running and blocking in a game. Nor have I heard students complaining about their teacher not doing their homework or exam for them. You are there to make heroes out of them. They know in their heart they will have to earn that credit themselves," the Mystic explained.

Scott wasn't all that sure. "I have difficulties envisioning that all the people in my client's team will accept what you propose."

"You may not be able to get acceptance from everyone, but you will always find champions," the Mystic explained. "Those who want to advance their career, who will become the future leaders of your client's organization, are the ones you should cultivate and help to become heroes."

Scott looked away from the Mystic while he digested this breakthrough thinking. He knew in his heart the knowledge conveyed to him today was precisely the solution. The brick walls he thought could not be scaled in the past seemed to be crumbling in front of him. He knew now that it was within his grasp to move his projects faster with higher customer satisfaction. Finally, he broke the silence.

"I believe the Lateral Approach to project management will work. I believe it is a win-win approach. How can I put this into practice?"
The Mystic walked up to the white board again and began writing:

Four On-Site Exercises
- **Create Your Own Success**
- **Assert Your Authority**
- **Empower Your Client**
- **Carry Out Your Leadership Role**

"Let's talk about this next."

Scott reflected on his conversation with the Mystic. He entered into his notebook the following:

Obtaining Acceptance

- The conventional approach to obtaining acceptance is by focusing on dotting the 'i's' and crossing the 't's. Lateral thinking challenges this approach because most contracts are grey.

- The conventional approach to obtaining acceptance, by focusing on dotting the 'i's' and crossing the 't's, often leads to disputes that risk client relations.

- The Lateral Approach to acceptance is more about confidence, deployment, and reaching agreements to move forward. It shouldn't be confrontational.

- When your clients go through the exercise to dot 'i's' and cross 't's' with you, they are, in fact, telling you that they do not have confidence in you, that they are not ready to deploy, and that they are not in agreement with you to move forward.

- Reaching an agreement to move forward with your clients implies willingness to trade-off, look ahead, become more practical, or adjust expectations.

- Gaining confidence and building the trust of your clients will not occur overnight. It is built up from the very beginning of the project.

- You gain confidence and trust from your clients by:
  - **Setting and Meeting Expectations**

o **Empowering Your Client for Flexibility and Change**

- Resetting expectations requires you to explain and clarify to your clients in the beginning and not at the end of the project what they have purchased.
- You can reset and meet expectations, build confidence and trust by following the principle of:
  o **SAY WHAT YOU DO and**
    DO WHAT YOU SAY
- Had you executed the first part of the principle, that is to SAY WHAT YOU DO, and your clients disagreed with you, your project could not have proceeded far.
- The two actions; SAY WHAT YOU DO and DO WHAT YOU SAY must go hand-in-hand. If you have to do what you say, you will be clearer and more careful with what you say in the first place. In fact, your first action is to reach agreement and reset expectations. The second action is to deliver against the promise and expectation. If you really follow this principle, you can be confident that you will meet your client's expectations.
- When you meet the expectations you set for your clients, they begin to have confidence and trust in you. That is a far cry from having confidence in taking over from you. Your shoes may be hard to fill from your clients' point-of-view.

- At the moment you ask for final acceptance, it is like a wake-up call for your clients that the responsibility for the system is passing from your hands to theirs. Suddenly, they will feel that they have not learned enough about the system to take on that responsibility. They are not so confident in themselves. It is less about you than about them.

- The empowerment process is a process of transferring ownership and educating your client starting from the beginning of the implementation process until final acceptance.

- You want your client's team to be able to say, "I know the system as much as you and I can take care of it from now on." When your client's team can say that, it means they have the knowledge and confidence to move forward alone. When they can say that, they will feel comfortable giving you the final acceptance you asked for.

- The empowerment process makes sense to anybody who understands the financial impact of having to pay each time something comes up. Your client surely doesn't want to be on-the-hook for your services or be held "hostage" by your services. Let your client know that empowerment is an important part of your mission at their site. It is a win-win approach.

- Many project managers mistakenly think that it is

their team's job to perform all the tasks and to deliver to clients a complete turn-key system. Until they learn the Lateral Approach, they don't realize that they are doing their clients a disservice as well as a disservice to themselves.

- When you do everything yourself, you deprive your client the opportunity to learn, and it becomes a lose-lose proposition. You are required to deploy more resources and in the end, both your work and the completed system are still a big mystery from your clients' perspective. Your client's team feels no ownership and no confidence.

- During the empowerment process, a lot depends on how you and your team conduct yourselves and lead the client's team. Instead of behaving like contract labor, you and your team should play the role of coaches and teachers. Football players never complain about their coach not doing the running and blocking in a game. Students never complain about their teacher not doing their home work or exam for them. You are there to make heroes out of them. They know in their hearts they have to earn that credit themselves.

- You will always find champions: those who want to advance their career. These people will become the future leaders of your clients' organization. Cultivate them and help them to become heroes.

- To put Lateral Approach project management into action:

  The Four On-Site Exercises
  - Create Your Own Success
  - Assert Your Authority
  - Empower Your Client
  - Carry Out Your Leadership Role

Chapter 6 – Exercise #1 - Create Your Own Success

Scott looked at the white board quite intensely, trying to grasp the significance of the four on-site exercises. He questioned what this was all about. He had never thought of his on-site work in terms of performing exercises. This wasn't how he had been taught.

The Mystic gave Scott a moment to digest the new information and then began asking him some questions.

"Scott, please tell me, what is your routine when you plan a client visit?"

"I usually set up my follow-up meeting during my last visit. I know some of my team members might or might not do that."

"That's good. What else?"

"Then I call or e-mail ahead to make sure my client is prepared for my visit. If needed, I adjust my schedule."

"That's good. What else?"

"If more than myself are visiting, my team and I normally have a huddle and coordinate what we will do at the meeting."

"Very good. What else?"

"Well, that's all I can think of," Scott finished.

The Mystic launched a new thought-provoking question. "Let me ask you this. How do you make sure, from your client's perspective, that your site visit will create value and be successful?"

"I don't understand. If I do my job, why shouldn't the site visit be valuable and successful?" Scott wasn't quite sure where the Mystic was leading him.

"Think about this: who will know and understand what you are doing while you are on-site?" the Mystic asked from a different perspective.

"The people we interact with, of course."

"What about those you might not have direct interaction with?" the Mystic pressed on, hoping that Scott would begin to think laterally about it.

"I don't know. Why would that be important?" Scott asked, surprised.

"You tell me. Would it be equally, if not more, important what the bosses, project sponsors, and decision makers think?"

"I guess it would, but wouldn't they be kept informed internally?"

"Perception can be their reality. Wouldn't you like them to be informed by you rather than having them rely on information fed to them by someone else?"

"Why would that be important?"

"It wouldn't as long as your project was going your way. In your case, it isn't, is it?" Once again, the Mystic was leading Scott to think laterally.

"No, it is not and now I don't think the people at the client site want me to communicate with their bosses, project sponsors, and decision makers,"

Scott answered, not fully realizing the significance of what he had just said.

"I wouldn't blame them," the Mystic agreed, making his point. "If I were them, I wouldn't want you to escalate a situation that might reflect badly on them. Neither would the bosses, project sponsors, and decision makers. They would distance themselves from you at this point."

"So what is your advice?" Scott asked, puzzled once again.

"The crux of on-site Exercise #1, Create Your Own Success, is to establish the channels and regularly communicate with your target audiences through these channels. Fortunately or unfortunately, your target audiences are normally not the people you work with day-in and day-out. Your target audiences are not visible unless you seek them out. They are the bosses, project sponsors, and decision makers who can either make or break the project," the Mystic explained.

"Wow, how do I reach these people?" Scott was beginning to see the importance.

"Timing is important. The opportunity to reach these people comes and goes. Normally there is an opportunity at the beginning of the project or at project re-start, like what you are facing now. Any time in between will send a different message. Sometimes even a casual conversation may be viewed as an escalation of the problem, and escalation is a sensitive matter," the Mystic replied.

"Why is it possible to accomplish this at the beginning of the project or at project re-start?"

The Mystic smiled and further explained the logic and approach. "It is all about making access and communication routine rather than incidental. We are all creatures of habit. We feel more comfortable with regularity and routine."

"So, how do I make interactions routine?"

"Now we come back to On-Site Exercise #1 and your site visit preparation. You cannot create your own success if you don't make and meet commitments and set challenging goals.

"You can create your own success by setting very specific and challenging goals in the form of an agenda that you know you can achieve. Then you must communicate these goals to your target audiences. In this case, as we agreed, your target audiences are really the bosses, project sponsors, and decision makers." The Mystic began to peel away and lay out the Lateral Approach.

"Is there a particular form of communication you recommend?"

"Interestingly, once you agree with me that the bosses, project sponsors, and decision makers are your real audiences; your method of communication naturally follows a certain pattern. That is the pattern of communication with senior managers who are always busy and short on time." The Mystic's answer was short and to the point.

"What would that mean?"

"I am glad you asked. That would mean, regardless of the complexity of your site visit agenda or goals, that you need to be able to explain them on no more than one to one-and-a-half pages of text. For face-to-face meetings, it means you request 15 minutes of meeting time or less," the Mystic replied. "I find 10 minutes is a good amount of time to request.

"These are the magic numbers. You will find that it takes work to communicate clearly within these constraints."

Scott was very surprised at such precision. "One to one-and-a-half pages and 15 minutes or less? How did you arrive at that?" Scott asked a little sarcastically.

The Mystic seemed to be expecting the question and his answer was well thought out. "I call these magic numbers because more than likely, your audiences will lose concentration if you exceed them. And any executive should find it hard to refuse a request for 10 minutes to meet with you during your site visit."

"I see. Very interesting! I have never thought about it from this perspective." The Lateral Approach was striking a cord with Scott.

"Remember, the key is to do it as part of a routine each time you visit a site. This is to create a pattern and a habit. This way, you establish a forum for regular communication and a rapport to build confidence and trust with your target audiences," the Mystic reinforced.

"What you just told me makes me realize the importance of a category of my work I have totally neglected before." Using the new lateral thinking, Scott was able to spot his own mistakes.

"Don't feel too badly, Scott. Chances are, many project managers never find out what they do not know. Those who do know eventually rise up to senior management positions."

The Mystic's encouragement further illustrated the importance of mastering the Lateral Approach and introduced its potential impact on Scott's future career potential. Now he really wanted to learn more.

"How would I initiate the routine in the first place?" he asked.

"Simple. Seek out these people and ask them for a 10-minute meeting," the Mystic answered with a smile.

"Then what?"

"In your meeting, introduce yourself and give your audience a quick status of the project. Then ask if they would like to be kept informed. Nine times out of 10, the person will say yes and thank you for asking," the Mystic assured him.

"What should I do in my case?" Scott wanted to verify.

"Tell the person you are meeting with how you would re-start the project, and ask if he or she would like to be kept informed. I can assure you that after what has happened so far with the project, that person will want to be kept informed. It is almost irresponsible not to want that. Then, make sure you take the time to always send a copy of your site visit agenda and updates to that person and make a point to drop by his or her office regularly as promised." The Mystic's words exuded confidence and helped convince Scott that he would be equally successful using this technique.

"Thank you," he said. "Now I know how to get started. On the other hand, I am still not sure how Exercise #1 can help me create success."

"So far, we have covered expanding the audiences you should be paying careful attention to. Exercise #1, Create Your Own Success, is about setting your agenda with objectives you can meet with certainty; putting into action the principle, SAY WHAT YOU DO and DO WHAT YOU SAY," the Mystic explained.

"What do you mean?"

The Mystic expanded. "It means doing a lot of preparation and planning so that you are absolutely confident you can accomplish the objectives that you set. It means leaving little to chance. Remember, building confidence and trust is about saying what you do and doing what you say you will do. In turn, you can expect others to do the same."

"But there is only so much you can do to prepare and plan." Scott was a little reluctant to agree completely. To him, it sounded like too much work for not much return.

"You know what, if you feel that way, either you should cancel your site visit or not include those objectives on your agenda." The Mystic wasn't happy with Scott's answer. He took on a stern expression.

Scott was a little taken back by the Mystic's response. He understood the seriousness of the Mystic's message and tried to respond positively. "I know what you mean."

"It will take work, but are you serious about wanting to be successful?"

"Yes I am, but I am not sure if I can succeed until I try." Scott gave an honest answer.

"That's all I am asking. Try it. The more you prepare and plan, the more you can be certain to succeed. The more you practice, the easier it becomes to do the preparation and planning. I believe you have the idea," the Mystic reassured.

"So, I do my homework and make sure my target audiences are fully informed and updated on the project. What am I really after?" Scott asked.

"Good question. You are after two simple things: three words and a signature." The Mystic gave a lateral answer but he didn't expect Scott to understand yet.

As expected, Scott was baffled. "Three words and a signature! What three words and what signature?"

"The three words are 'Let's go live' and the signature is your client's name on your referral letter to your next prospective customer. Remember, going live is a nervous time. You need the people at the top to have the confidence and trust that you will stand by them as they take on final responsibility. Having your client be a reference for future prospects is worth more than money to your company.

"Is all this coming together and making sense?" The Mystic wasn't holding back and wanted to tell Scott everything he intended.

Scott's face lit up. "It makes a lot of sense now," he said, nodding his head. Finally, Scott seemed to see the whole picture.

Scott reflected on his conversation with the Mystic. He entered into his notebook the following:

Create Your Own Success

- Perception can be the reality. It can be equally if not more important what the client's bosses, project sponsors, decision makers think of the value and successes you bring. You should choose to keep them informed instead of relying on someone else to do it.

- It may not matter who does the informing as long as your project is going well. It matters a lot when something goes wrong.

- When a project goes wrong, people don't want you to communicate with their bosses, project sponsors, and decision makers. Your communication would be viewed as escalation, which might reflect badly on them. Bosses, project sponsors, and decision makers also want to distance themselves from you.

- In order to gain access and communicate directly with the client's bosses, project sponsors, and decision makers, Lateral Approach project management creates an environment that can make the interaction a matter of routine rather than an incident.

- We are all creatures of habit. We feel more comfortable with regularity and routine.

- The crux of On-Site Exercise #1, Create Your Own Success, is to establish the channels and communicate regularly with your target audiences through these channels.

- Fortunately or unfortunately, your target audiences are normally not the people you work with day-in and day-out. Your target audiences are not visible unless you seek them out.

- You cannot create your own success if you don't make and meet commitments and set challenging goals. You can create your own success by setting very specific challenging goals in the form of an agenda that you know you can achieve. Then you must communicate these goals to your target audiences.

- The Lateral Approach says that your target audiences are really the client's bosses, project sponsors, and decision makers.

- The Lateral Approach magic number on reports is one to one-and-a-half pages. More than that and chances are your audiences will lose concentration.

- The Lateral Approach magic number on scheduling meetings is for 15 minutes. Ten to 15-minute meeting requests are hard to refuse.

- The Lateral Approach to establishing routine meetings is to ask in your first meeting if the client would like to be kept informed. Nine times out of 10, the person will say yes and thank you for asking.

- Exercise #1- Create Your Own Success is about setting your agenda and objectives so you can meet them with certainty; putting into action the principle SAY WHAT YOU DO and DO WHAT YOU SAY.

- Building confidence and trust is about saying what you do and doing what you say you will do. In turn, you can expect others to do the same.

- The more you prepare and plan, the more you can be certain to succeed. The more you practice, the easier it becomes to prepare and plan.

- Going live is a nervous time. You need the people at the top to have confidence and trust that you will stand by them in order for them to take on the final responsibility.

Chapter 7 – Exercise #2 - Assert Your Authority

Scott felt that he had just learned something new and important from listening to the Mystic about the exercise for creating success. He was now very curious about the next exercise, what the Mystic called, Assert Your Authority.

He said, "Thanks for explaining the implications and the process around creating success. I wouldn't have thought about it as a regular exercise. I can't wait to know more about the next on-site exercise – assert your authority."

"Well, why don't you tell me what asserting authority means to you?" the Mystic began.

"If I were to interpret it literally, it tells me to take charge of my team, doesn't it?" Scott replied.

"Before I answer, tell me who is on your team," the Mystic asked.

"All the resources assigned to me that I have authority over, right?" By the way the Mystic had asked the question, Scott felt that there was

113

probably more to the question than what he had answered.

"Well, what would that include?" the Mystic prompted.

"What do you mean what would that include? I only have authority over those resources assigned to me by my company. That is the extent of my authority."

"Is that really true? Then let me also ask you what you are responsible for."

"I am responsible for the success of the project," Scott quickly answered.

"Absolutely! Now you're talking. That is what your client hired you for. What does that responsibility make you?" the Mystic encouraged.

"It makes me lose sleep at night." Scott hoped that humor would cover his ignorance of what the Mystic was looking for.

Trying not to embarrass Scott, the Mystic smiled and continued. "That would make you the leader of the project, wouldn't it? As the leader, you bear the full responsibility for the success of the project. That may be why you lose sleep over it. With full responsibility, you actually have the full authority over all the resources involved in the project. Do you know that?" Finally, the Mystic explained what he meant and backed up his explanation with business logic.

"What do you mean by the full authority?" Scott asked disbelievingly.

"I mean you have the full authority over both your company's and your client's resources," the Mystic replied with confidence.

"No, that cannot be." Scott was reluctant to accept the answer.

"Why not?" the Mystic challenged.

"The client's resources are managed by my client. I don't manage my client resources." Scott expressed his own version of business logic.

"Do you mean you have been managing half of your projects? Do you mean you are denying your responsibility for leading this project to success?"

"That is not what I meant," Scott said, defending his answer.

The Mystic gave Scott the opportunity to clarify. "That is what I am hearing. What then do you really mean?"

"I mean I don't have the authority over our client because my boss always told me, 'customer is king' and 'customer is always right'. My client has authority over me and not the other way around, it seems to me," Scott explained.

"Ah. You just brought up a most common misconception. When your boss said that the 'customer is king' or 'customer is always right', or even 'you serve at the pleasure of your client', your boss was referring to meeting your customer's needs and providing excellent and flexible service. Your boss wasn't asking you to be unprofessional about your role.

"As a professional and a leader, you accepted the responsibility and, therefore, the corresponding authority. Do you understand the difference?" The Mystic tried to cut right through Scott's tangled misconception.

"It may be authority and leadership in name but not in fact. What authority do I really have?" Scott still wasn't sure. After all, he had operated under his belief about what 'customer is king' meant for a long time.

"It all depends on how you behave as a leader and how you assert your authority," the Mystic replied. "You have more authority than you think. That is why you need to learn how to assert your authority by practicing on-site Exercise #2."

The Mystic seemed to understand Scott's struggle. He slowly led Scott to the lateral way of thinking and away from his old misconceptions.

"I see. It comes around to the on-site exercise. So how do I assert my authority when I cannot reward or punish?"

"Management and leadership and the corresponding authority aren't about title or position. It is about influencing people so that they want to listen to you, accept your opinions, and follow your instructions," the Mystic began to explain.

"I don't get it."

"Imagine you are commanding a thousand people. You can command not because you are reaching down and managing every last person. You are managing through a chain of command. You are working with your most trusted people. Do you follow?"

"Yes, so far," Scott acknowledged hesitantly.

"If you rely on the chain of command and on your most trusted people, and even though you have the authority to hire and fire and reward and punish, you will only punish or fire someone on very rare occasions. Why?" the Mystic prompted.

"Why?" Scott asked.

"Because your authority and power come from having your trusted few listen to you, accept your opinions, and follow your instruction. You don't want to cut off your own right arm unless it is absolutely necessary. Almost always, you will lead with rewards and praise. You can't lead or motivate from the gutter. Ultimately, you will not be the one to either reward or punish, hire or fire. You will leave such tasks to those you trust or those who trust you.

"In the case of your client, by having access to and an ongoing relationship with their senior management, you have influence. That is all you need. As such, reward and punishment need not necessarily be by your own hand. Do you get it now?" The Mystic explained the deeper concept of people management with respect to reward and punishment.

"Oh. I didn't realize that. So the actual act of rewarding or punishing, hiring or firing, isn't as important as I thought. Praise that might lead to rewards becomes the most important management tool." Scott was starting to catch on to the leadership principle the Mystic was talking about.

"You've got it. Understanding what I just told you will help put you on top of the management chain. You must lead with positive incentives. People will tend to listen and follow you once they have enjoyed the rewards of your praise," the Mystic summarized.

"How does that apply to project management and the Assert Your Authority exercise?" Scott wanted to know.

"Remember, in Exercise #1 you are to establish regular meetings with the client's bosses, project sponsors, and decision makers. Bring your client's project manager with you. In this meeting, you will be asserting your authority," the Mystic started explaining.

Scott was a little puzzled. Expecting that response, the Mystic continued.

"Imagine the following scenario. The meeting is attended by three parties or more: the client's boss, the client's project managers, and you. There are four parts to this meeting. First, since you called the meeting, you should start the meeting by asking the client's project manager to give a project status summary to his boss. You are there to make sure that all the accomplishments are covered. Any questions so far?" The Mystic gestured as if he was conducting a virtual meeting.

"Why shouldn't I be the one to give the project status?"

"Good question. You could, but as part of asserting your authority, it is better if you ask the client's project manager to give the status. The exercise to exert your authority begins with you providing instruction and having the client's project manager respond to your instruction.

"Besides, if the project status comes from your client's project manager, then it is the client's own perspective on the status," the Mystic explained, diving into the finer details of the application of the Lateral Approach.

"Makes sense to start with a simple request," Scott agreed. "So what comes next?" He was getting it now.

"The second and very important part is to give the client's project manager a pat on the back and your sincere praise, recognition, and appreciation for him and his team."

"I follow. We touched on this subject earlier. So what is next?" Scott asked, becoming a little impatient.

"The third part is to say a few words about what you plan to accomplish on your next visit. Then assert your authority again by looking the project manager in the eye to reiterate what you expect him to accomplish before your next visit. You are talking about his expected work and not yours. You are reiterating because both of you should have talked about the subject before the meeting."

"Is that it?" Scott was surprised at the simplicity of it all, but was quickly informed that there was more to come.

"No," the Mystic said. "The fourth step is to conclude the exercise by looking around at each person in the meeting to see if there are disagreements on the project status and the objectives for the next visit. Resolve all matters in this meeting until all parties are in agreement, and then adjourn the meeting. If you have done your job in Exercise #1, Create Your Own Success, there should be little or no disagreement."

He continued, "The meeting should not last more than 15 to 20 minutes. Within that time you will have assigned authority to yourself through the manner in which you conducted and concluded the meeting. On occasion, I have even used such an opportunity to hand our client a bill." The Mystic said this with a laugh. Scott also laughed because he knew getting his client to sign off on paying invoices was sometimes something of a challenge. He was also bewildered, as the Mystic fully expected.

"I don't get it," he asked. "How will this bring authority to me?"

"Here is what actually transpired. When you held the meeting with your client's boss, your unspoken words to your client's project manager were, 'I have access to your boss.' Having access translates to power." The Mystic was taking pleasure at unpeeling the first layers of this lateral puzzle.

Scott listened intently as the Mystic continued.

"When you patted the project manager on the back, the unspoken words were, 'I can give praise, but there is no guarantee my praise will continue if you don't perform.' The praise just helped shift the client project manager's focus on demonstrating performance with respect to reward and punishment from his boss to you." The Mystic smiled as he peeled back the second layer of the lateral puzzle.

"Umm, I am beginning to see where you are heading." Scott nodded his head as he started to catch on.

123

"When you lay out in front of the client's boss your expectations and assignments for the project manager for your next visit, the unspoken words to the client manager were, 'Speak up now or forever hold your peace.' When the boss kept quiet while you handed out instructions and expectations, he blessed the assertion of your authority. Therefore, the exercise brought authority to you.

"Do you now see what was going on?" The Mystic looked for Scott's reaction as he unpeeled the final layer of the lateral puzzle.

"That's cool. You have just opened my eyes," Scott broke out joyfully. What he thought could not be done now seemed so simple and obvious.

"As you see, there is no title or corporate boundaries involved when it comes to leadership," the Mystic reaffirmed.

Scott felt more confident and was eager to try out the exercise. He had held those three-party meetings before. He had also praised project managers in front of their bosses. Without being conscious of the impact and effect, he felt that he had let opportunities pass him by. Now he felt enlightened and was confident he would be in much better control of the success of his projects going forward.

Scott reflected on his conversation with the Mystic. He entered into his notebook the following:

Assert Your Authority

- According to the Lateral Approach, it is a common misconception that a client's resources are managed by your client and that you have no authority to manage your client's resources. This misconception tends to make project managers manage only half of a project.

- As the project leader, you bear the full responsibility for the success of the project. With full responsibility, you actually have the full authority over all the resources involved in the project.

- When your boss said that 'customer is king', or 'customer is always right', or even 'you are serving at the pleasure of your client', your boss was referring to meeting your customer's needs and providing excellent and flexible services. He wasn't asking you to be unprofessional about your role.

- You have more authority than you think. That is why you need to practice asserting your authority as a regular on-site exercise.

- Management and leadership and the corresponding authority aren't about title or position. It is about influencing people so that they will want to listen to you, accept your opinions, and follow your

instructions.
- **Assert Your Authority Meeting** (3 Parties and 4 Steps)
    - Step 1 – Ask the client project manager to give a 10-minute project status to his boss.
    - Step 2 – Give the client project manager a pat on his back along with your sincere praise, recognition, and appreciation to his team.
    - Step 3 – Say a few words about what you plan to accomplish on your next trip. Then assert your authority by reiterating what you expect to see from the client project manager before your next visit.
    - Step 4 – Conclude the exercise by giving everyone an opportunity for input on the project status and the objective for the next visit. Resolve all disagreements, if any, on the spot.
- The Lateral Approach translates the three-party meeting with your client's boss into the unspoken words: 'I have access to your bosses.' Having access is power.
- The Lateral Approach translates the pat on the client project manager's back into the unspoken words: 'I can give praise, but there is no guarantee my praise will continue if you don't perform.' The praise just

helps you shift the client project manager's focus on showing performance with respect to reward and punishment from his boss to you.

- The Lateral Approach translates your action of laying out in front of the client's boss your expectations and assignments for the client project manager into the unspoken words: 'speak up now or forever hold your peace.' When the client's boss keeps quiet while you are handing out instructions and expectations, he just blessed the assertion of your authority. Therefore, the exercise brought authority to you.

Chapter 8 – Exercise #3 - Empower Your Clients

By this time, Scott had begun to understand the power of the Lateral Approach to project management. Lateral thinking was very different from what he was used to. As the exercises unfolded, each step seemed to make a lot of sense. Each step seemed easy enough for him to practice and master.

Now Scott was anxious to get to Exercise #3, Empower Your Client. Empowerment was such a common practice in management nowadays that he felt that he knew what it was all about. On the other hand, empowering your client? That seemed a little weird.

"I don't get it," Scott asked the Mystic. "What is this exercise about? What do you mean by empowering your client? How do I give power to our client?"

As always, rather than answer Scott's question directly, the Mystic tried to lead Scott to first think it through.

129

"Before I answer your question, can you tell me what the mission of your project is?"
Scott gave his standard answer. "My mission is to implement the new system and train the users so that our client's company can benefit from using it."

"Right! Not only do you want your system to be implemented, you also want the people to know the system well enough so that they don't have to call you up about every single thing," the Mystic acknowledged.

"That's right," Scott concurred.

"In other words, you want to empower your client to be flexible and able to respond to change," the Mystic reiterated.

"You could say that." Scott was not exactly sure of the Mystic's interpretation but felt that it was similar to what he had said.

"Guess what this really means?" the Mystic queried.

"What?" Scott was not quite sure.

"It means that the more you do for your client that they can do for themselves, the more you are depriving the client of the opportunity to learn and be empowered."

"What do you mean? Are you saying I should do less for my client?" Now Scott was no longer sure he agreed with the Mystic in the first place.

"Focus on the result. Getting more done with less is what you are after. You are to do as much as necessary. Doing more for the sake of doing more does not mean you accomplish more," the Mystic explained further. But Scott continued to be totally lost.

"How can I get my client to accept what you are proposing?" To Scott, it seemed illogical and impossible.

The Mystic prompted Scott to think laterally, saying, "If you explain the concept properly to the client's senior management, they will certainly accept it."

"How would you explain it to them?"

"I would explain it by saying that your mission is to empower their people to handle all kinds of situations. You don't want your client to have to call you for consultation each time a new situation arises, because it will cost them.

"I would explain that you can accomplish your mission by not depriving their staff of the opportunity to learn while you are there to support them during your engagement. That means your clients should learn on the job, get their hands dirty, and do what they can do. You are there to help them practice, to do what they do not yet know how to do."

"I'll buy that. What do I tell the staff who has to do the work?"

"You don't tell them anything. You just perform the empowerment exercise," the Mystic said simply.

"What would that be?"

"It can be anything."

"Anything?" Scott looked at the Mystic disbelievingly.

"Yes, anything that your client can do, you should not do," the Mystic explained. "For example, if you have to train 100 users and you have trained the first 10, the next 30 users should be trained by a select few from the first 10. You stand by and coach. You are to cheer, encourage, praise, and guide the new trainers. Then, a select few from the first 40 trained users and trainers should train the balance of the 60 users. That is an empowerment exercise."

"Now I am starting to get it," said Scott, giving in a little more.

"If you think carefully through the empowerment exercise, you will see the multiple benefits," the Mystic continued.

"What are these benefits?"

"First of all, you changed the training environment in which people sit back with their arms folded, challenging you to get them trained," the Mystic explained.

"Yes. Those situations are not uncommon," Scott agreed.

"The empowerment exercise turned your client from a passive receiver to an owner of the training program."

"That is important," Scott agreed.

"Encourage your client trainers to add their own local domain knowledge to the training program. This way, they are invested in training their peers successfully. And when they do, they will take pride in their accomplishment and feel ownership of the system," the Mystic summarized.

"That is big." Scott acknowledged the breakthrough.

"Buy-in becomes almost automatic," the Mystic added.

"That's the name of the game," Scott agreed.

"Of course, this example is about training. The same can apply to system set-up, installation, data collection, and more." The Mystic made sure Scott understood how the empowerment exercise could extend to every aspect of the project.

"I think I have it." Scott felt satisfied.

Scott reflected on his conversation with the Mystic. He entered into his notebook the following:

Empower Your Client

- Your mission is to empower your client for flexibility and change. Not only have do you want your system to be implemented; you also want the client's team to know the system well enough so that they don't have to call you up for every single thing.

- Empowering your client in project management means the more you do for your client what they can do for themselves, the more you are depriving the client the opportunity to learn and be empowered.

- You are to do as much as necessary. Doing more for the sake of doing more does not mean you accomplish more.

- The Lateral Approach requires you to explain to your client's senior management that your mission is to empower their people so that they do not have to call you or your firm for consultation each time a new situation arises and incur additional cost. You can accomplish your mission by not depriving their staff the opportunity to learn while you are there to support them during your engagement. That means your clients should learn on the job, get their hands dirty and do what they can do. You are there to help them practice and learn to do what they do not yet

135

know how to do.

- Empowerment exercises turn your clients from passive receivers into owners of the project.

Chapter 9 – Exercise #4 - Carry Out Your Leadership Role

The Mystic took a long look at Scott. He was nodding his head with approval. Not so long ago, Scott had been grim and discouraged. Now, he seemed to have regained his enthusiasm and confidence. He had become a new person with a new mission. It showed in his attitude and disposition. While Scott was busy writing down his notes, the Mystic broke the silence.

"Shall we move on?"

"Yes, I want very much to know what Carry Out Your Leadership Role is about," Scott answered.

"First, I would like to hear what you think."

"Well, several times you mentioned leadership and the value of leadership. You mentioned that my client is actually paying a lot of money for leadership. And that leadership may even be more important than our products or services," Scott recalled.

"That is all true. How well you earn your keep depends on how well you handle adversities and problems. That is when leadership counts. A dummy can handle projects if the projects have no problems, but that's unlikely. The question is, how would you demonstrate your leadership skills?"

"That is hard to say. Either you have them or you don't," Scott replied, a little caught off guard.

"That is not true," the Mystic countered. "Given the opportunities, everyone can become a leader. By recognizing that leadership skills are within all of us, we can cultivate this strength for project management purposes," he explained.

"Oh! Is that so?" Scott was not fully convinced.

"People often are mistaken that project management is just work. It is much more than work, especially if it includes managing projects that involve many people who each have their own personal interests."

"You're telling me!" Scott recognized that he had been there before.

"To begin, your leadership role is to help all the people impacted by your project to have clear visions, goals, and objectives and to inspire them to do extraordinary things," the Mystic explained.

"I know, and I thought I had been spelling out visions, goals, and objectives at the start of each project already. Even for this failed project, both my boss and my client's boss came to talk about it at project kick-off. It doesn't seem to have helped this time." Scott was somewhat confused.

"I believe you. That is why carrying out your leadership role is an ongoing exercise. It is not a one-time thing. It is needed each time you interact with your client and staff. That is why I call it an exercise. It is not an event. It is a regular exercise!"

"Why is that?" Scott asked, feeling more frustrated.

The Mystic explained calmly. "Try to put yourself in the shoes of all the people involved. After a project starts, when the excitement is gone and the real work begins to take its toll, how much do you think people remember about the original message and vision? How much do the visions, goals, and objectives matter to them then?"

"I understand. I have heard those complaints." Scott found he agreed with the Mystic on this point.

"Why do you think they complained?" the Mystic asked without hesitation.

"They seemed to complaint about everything," Scott answered.

"Chances are things were changing, and the end of the road seemed too far away and too difficult to reach. Chances are they may not have understood what was in it for them, and they may have felt that, in the end, they would be left holding the short end of the stick. Did you find that to be true?" the Mystic asked, explaining some of the root causes of these kinds of complaints.

"I believe that doubt may have played a role, but that didn't seem to be all." The Mystic's answer hadn't satisfied Scott totally.

The Mystic patiently attempted to help Scott break through. "True, in order to lead, people must be willing to follow. In order for people to follow you, they need to see a torch, a vision. If you are the one holding the torch that is leading and lighting the way, they must trust and believe in you and your direction. They must be willing to take a chance with you. Can you imagine what you would need to do in order to earn that trust?"

"I am not sure." Scott was trying but he wasn't there yet.

"If you want people to follow, you must grab every opportunity to make them feel safe. You must demonstrate your willingness to take responsibility when things go wrong. You must be absolutely honest and talk straight. You must seek out opportunities to show sincere respect and appreciation and give praise. You must demonstrate you know what you are doing. All these are no small tasks," the Mystic explained further.

"How do I do all that?"

Scott's question didn't surprise the Mystic, and it gave him another chance to explain in greater detail. "Let me tell you this. Throughout the project cycle, there will be no lack of opportunities to carry out your leadership role. Unfortunately, many project managers aren't trained to recognize and make the best use of these opportunities.

Therefore, they miss opportunities without knowing it. The leadership exercise is to help cultivate and strengthen this skill within all of us."

"This is good to know, but when people start complaining, how do I carry out my leadership role?"

"If you accept your leadership role and the exercise, every situation becomes an opportunity for you. In the case of complaints, you must begin as a good listener. You must hear what people are really saying. This is an opportunity for you to be honest and straightforward. Keep in mind, normally there are two sides to everything. Your role as leader is to always view the glass as half-full instead of half-empty. Your role is to give hope and stay optimistic."

Scott was hearing what the Mystic was saying but wanted to take the opportunity to ask about a common occurrence in project management. He asked, "But when people complain and don't do their part of the assigned work, the project progress gets delayed and costs escalate. How can I stay optimistic and give praise in such a situation?"

"That is a good question. At first glance, you would wonder how something seemingly so negative could be viewed as positive, right? In fact, the situation you described goes deeper. Why don't you first ask yourself who you think is really responsible?"

"If my people and I have done our part and the client has not done theirs, then obviously, they are responsible for not fulfilling their responsibilities and causing the project delays." Scott gave the answer the Mystic had expected.

He said, "From a leadership responsibility viewpoint, you may have to think again. If you view yourself as the true leader of the project, there is no more 'our part versus their part'; not anymore! There is only the project. If you are responsible for the project, you are responsible regardless of who did what. Do you understand?"

"I don't understand how taking responsibility for their failure helps me become a better leader." Once again, Scott responded as the Mystic had expected.

"Aah. It helps a lot! By listening to the complaints of your people, regardless of who they are, and taking responsibility for project failures, regardless of the cause, you demonstrate your leadership. The message to everyone is that you are willing to be the shield for everyone; that you will protect them while they do their part; that they can feel safe standing behind you.

"Because you took the responsibility, it gave you the opportunity to reiterate the original visions, goals, and objectives that will benefit everyone, not just your own staff. While it is not a time for praise, a setback gives you the opportunity to inspire and show appreciation for people's efforts. You also can use the opportunity to point out everyone's strengths, abilities, and potential. Are you following?"

"Yes, so far so good!" Scott responded.

"Let us take the Lateral Approach further," the Mystic continued. "You can also show appreciation and respect even for those who may have disappointed you. This is not to endorse their failure to perform or to deliver. It is an exercise in empowering yourself to reset expectations and consolidate commitments."

Scott was thrilled as the things the Mystic was talking about all started to make sense. "Wow, that's definitely not my usual reaction to failure. What you are saying is giving me a totally new perspective."

"Taking responsibility and showing sincere appreciation and respect isn't an easy path. But that's what differentiates a true leader," the Mystic cautioned.

Scott wanted further clarification. "Let me ask you something else."

"Go ahead," the Mystic encouraged.

"Earlier on, I asked about vision. Often the vision feels so remote for many people. People may not be able to relate to it. As vision may involve change, some may feel insecure. As a result, the project may not get a fair chance to come to completion or to realize its benefits. How would you handle that?"

"That is the challenge for most project managers. It is also where the leadership exercise comes in handy. As the leader of the project, you cannot assume that people fully understand or appreciate its vision. Like you said, some may feel insecure.

When people don't understand, it is, in fact, your opportunity to further explain as well as to inspire."

"How?" Scott asked.

"As you said, people may not be able to relate to the vision or certain goals, objectives, or benefits of their work. Your job is to explain it all in different ways that lead to the same conclusions. Your job is to explain in simple terms that they can relate to.

"Your job is to assign work where success is not far away but within easy grasp," the Mystic further explained.

"Why would that be important?"

"It is important to inspire people to do work where success is within grasp. In this respect, people are actually moving toward the same vision, goals, and objectives even though they may not fully understand or believe in them. In order to inspire, you need to come at it many times in many ways. That is why it becomes a regular exercise," the Mystic answered.

"Will that really work?" Scott questioned.

"Of course! Some people may not understand all the elements of a project but, in most cases, they will be willing to give the project a chance. They may also be more reserved than you might hope for or expect, but that brings you back to doing the leadership exercise regularly. You need to repeat it many times throughout a project."

Scott wanted to explore another common encounter he had experienced. "As you mentioned, leadership skills are in all of us. Often, I find that many people want to lead the project in their own way. Some people may not want to participate unless they are the ones calling the shots. What should I do then?"

"To begin with, the position of project leader may not be the most envious to be in. Some people may not understand that the one who stands in that position will likely lose sleep because the responsibilities are so heavy," the Mystic began.

"I know. Especially when things aren't going the way you hope or expect," Scott acknowledged.

"As leader, you want to embrace everyone who has leadership skills. That will build a strong team.

There are plenty of leadership positions to go around," the Mystic advised.

Scott wanted to dig deeper. "Can my position be shared?"

"Good question," the Mystic answered. "The real answer is no. There will be times when decisions can be complex, with no clear answers. Nonetheless, someone has to judge, make the decisions, and take action. With this in mind, sharing leadership would be confusing, with no one really taking on full responsibility. Having said that, the process used to arrive at decisions that can be shared, discussed, and debated openly." The Mystic seemed quite definitive in this respect.

"I find that open discussions and debates often lead to people taking sides. What leadership exercise can help to resolve this situation?"

The Mystic offered a lateral solution. "It would be idealistic to expect everyone to share your opinion. It is healthy to have opposing views. Sometimes, when the opposing view may be wrong but in your judgment not important or critical, you might let it be and treat it as a learning exercise for the team.

Many people often make the mistake of fighting unnecessary fights and for the wrong reasons. Sometimes, it is better not to win some fights and debates."

Using the Mystic's lateral thinking solution, Scott could suddenly see the benefits. "What I am hearing is, focus on getting to the destination. By not winning every debate and being more willing to try alternative approaches, you allow people to embrace visions, goals, and objectives on their own terms. They may even begin to own the project in stronger terms."

"You've got it." The Mystic was very happy that Scott was able to embrace this point, knowing that many people, especially those with strong egos, can get tripped up over it.

"I am beginning to see the power of the exercise." Scott was happy also and it showed in his attitude.

"I am glad to hear this from you," the Mystic further encouraged.

"Let me make sure and summarize the leadership exercise. First of all, it is an exercise that needs to be carried out throughout the project." Feeling excited, Scott was happy to show off what he learned.

"You've got it." The Mystic nodded his head in acknowledgement.

"Opportunities to carry out the leadership role are plenty. It is my job to seek out these opportunities," Scott continued with enthusiasm.

"You've got it." The Mystic continued his endorsement.

"In order to make people understand and embrace the vision, I need to come at it in many ways and many times," Scott continued.

"Yes."

"In order to hold the torch and lead the way, I must build trust." Scott was speaking faster now.

"Yes." The Mystic was smiling and nodding his agreement.

"To build trust, people must feel safe standing behind me," Scott continued.

"You've got it."

"To make people feel safe, I need to take responsibility for any failure of the project regardless of cause," Scott continued, smiling to himself.

"Yes." The Mystic gave Scott a thumbs-up.

"To inspire people to do extraordinary things, I must show appreciation and respect. I must make people believe that they can make a difference." Scott acknowledged the Mystic's encouragement with his own thumbs-up.

"Yes!" the Mystic responded definitively.

"From this respect, project management is no longer just work. My role and my job is to show the direction and inspire people to work toward our vision, goals, and objectives." Scott spoke with relief as he made his last point.

"That is it!" The Mystic broke into a cheer and started clapping. Scott was so happy with himself, he clapped along. Both ended up patting each other on the shoulders.

"Scott, you are ready. Go back and turn this project around!" The Mystic pointed at the door.

"Yes, Sir and thank you, Sir." Scott gave the Mystic a salute, happy to oblige.

Scott reflected on his conversation with the Mystic. He entered into his notebook the following:

Carry Out Your Leadership Role

- How you earn your keep depends on how well you handle adversities and problems. That is when leadership counts.

- Given the opportunities, everyone can become a leader. By recognizing that leadership skills are within all of us, we can cultivate this strength for project management purposes.

- People often are mistaken that project management is just work. It is much more than work, especially when managing projects that involve many people, each with their own private interests.

- Your leadership role is to help all the people impacted by your project to have clear visions, goals, and objectives and inspire them to do extraordinary things.

- Carrying out your leadership role is an ongoing and on-site exercise. It is not a one- time thing. It is needed each time you interact with your clients and their staff.

- After a project starts, when the excitement is gone and real project work begins to take its toll, your audience and your people won't remember the original message, and the visions, goals, and objectives won't matter to them.

- When people complain, chances are things are changing, and the end of the road seems so far away and so difficult to reach. Chances are they may not understand what is in it for them, and they may feel that at the end, they may be left holding the short end of the stick.

- In order to lead, people must be willing to follow you. In order for people to follow you, they need to see a torch, a vision. You are the one holding the torch leading and lighting the way.

- In order to lead, people must trust and believe in you and your direction as they follow you and the torch. They must be willing to take a chance with you.

- If you want people to follow, you must grab every opportunity to make them feel safe. You must demonstrate your willingness to take responsibility when things go wrong. You must be absolutely honest and talk straight. You must seek out opportunities to show sincere respect and appreciation and give praise. You must demonstrate you know what you are doing. All these are no small tasks.

- Throughout the project cycle, there will be no lack

of opportunities to carry out your leadership role. Unfortunately, many project managers aren't trained to recognize and make the best use of these opportunities. Therefore, they miss these opportunities without knowing it.

- If you accept your leadership role and the exercise, every situation becomes an opportunity for you.

- There are two sides to everything. Your role as leader is to always view the glass as half-full instead of half-empty. Your role is to give hope and stay optimistic.

- If you view yourself as the true leader of the project, there is no more 'our part versus their part'; not anymore! There is only the project. If you are responsible for the project, you are the responsible party regardless of who does what.

- By listening to the complaints of your people regardless of who they are, and taking responsibility for project failures regardless of cause, you demonstrate your leadership. The message to everyone is that you are willing to be the shield for everyone. You will protect them while they do their part. They can feel safe standing behind you.

- Because you took the responsibility, that gave you the opportunity to reiterate the original visions, goals, and objectives that benefit everyone. While it is not a time for praise, temporary failure is also an opportunity to inspire and show appreciation for people's efforts. You also should use the opportunity to point out everyone's strengths, abilities, and potential.

- You may show appreciation and respect even for those who may have disappointed you. This is not to endorse failure to perform or to deliver. It is an exercise in empowering yourself to reset expectations and consolidate commitments.

- As the leader of the project, you cannot assume that people fully understand or appreciate a vision. Some may feel insecure. When people don't understand, it is, in fact, your opportunity to further explain as well as to inspire.

- Your job is to explain different ways for getting to the same destination. Your job is to explain in simple terms that people can relate to. Your job is to assign work where success is not far away, but rather, within grasp.

- It is important to inspire people to do work where success is within grasp. In this respect, people are actually moving toward the same vision, goals, and objectives even though they may not fully understand or believe in them. In order to inspire, you need to come at it many times in many ways. That is why it becomes a regular exercise.

- Some people may not understand the vision, goals, and objectives of your project, but in most case, people will give your project a chance.
- As leader, you should embrace everyone with leadership skills. That will build a strong team. There are plenty of leadership positions to go around.
- It would be idealistic to expect everyone to share your opinion. It is healthy to have opposing views.
- Sometimes, when the opposing view may be wrong, but in your judgment it isn't important or critical, you might let it be and treat it as a learning exercise for the rest of the people. Many people often make the mistake of fighting unnecessary fights and for the wrong reasons. It is better for you not to win some fights and debates.
- By not winning every debate and being more willing to try alternative approaches, you are, in fact, allowing people to embrace the vision, goals, and objectives on their own terms. They may even own the project in stronger terms.

- **My Leadership Exercise**:
    - The leadership exercise is an exercise that needs to be carried out throughout the project.
    - Opportunities to carry out the leadership role are plenty. It is my job to seek out these opportunities.
    - In order to make people understand and embrace the vision, I need to come at it in many ways and many times.
    - To hold the torch and lead the way, I must build trust.
    - To build trust, people must feel safe standing behind me.
    - To make people feel safe, I need to take responsibility for any failure of the project, regardless of cause.
    - To inspire people to do extraordinary things, I must show appreciation and respect. I must make people believe that they can make a difference.
    - From this respect, project management is no longer just work-work. My role and my job is to show direction and inspire people to work toward our vision.
-

Chapter 10 – Customer Satisfaction

Scott walked apprehensively into John's office. He wasn't quite sure why he had been asked to go there and remembered how his previous experience had not been the most pleasant. He knew that the Mystic had encouraged John to give him another shot at the project. Scott thought the project was doing well now. As far he was concerned, the clients had responded positively.

John greeted Scott with a smile and extended his hand.

"Scott, what have you done at Johnson's Pharmaceutical?" John asked curiously.

"Well, I am just doing my best." Now Scott was becoming even more apprehensive.

John tried to put Scott at ease, saying, "No, no, no. You have done better than that. They seem to love you over there."

"Oh, I really didn't do much. In fact, I feel I have done less than before, yet the project is moving more smoothly," Scott responded.

"Our clients have a lot of good things to say about you and your leadership. They aren't sure exactly what happened, but their project staff and most employees involved are all standing behind you and supporting you and the project." John related what he had heard from the clients.

"That is probably the result of the four on-site exercises I am practicing nowadays. The Mystic taught me that," Scott responded.

"The last thing I expected from Johnson's Pharmaceutical was an expansion of the contract. I just got a call from them. Instead of complaining about how much money they have spent, they feel that they are getting their money's worth and the project is paying off in financial terms. So, they want more. How were you able to do that?" John was having a little difficulty suppressing his surprise.

"Oh that! I did make a conscious effort to create value by pointing out what they are getting. Once they realized the true value, they saw that what we are charging is a bargain. I didn't expect them to expand the project as I suggested, though." Scott was also somewhat surprised that his clients had followed his suggestion.

"I can see the reason why. Once our clients realized that they can get a good return on their investment, it makes a lot of sense to invest more. I would have done the same thing," John responded.

"That's good to know," Scott nodded.

John had more good news to share. "You may not know that our accounting department is happy also. Johnson's Pharmaceutical seems to be paying their bills on time. Their payment schedule is meeting our own cash flow projection. How did you do that?"

"Looking back, it wasn't so hard. Once I accepted the reality that most contracts are grey and I gained my client's trust, we ended up working together and helping each other. We stopped the practice of crossing 'i's' and dotting 't's' when it came to meeting contractual obligations. Both sides became more practical in meeting our objectives. Sign-off's and acceptance became a simple matter of coming to an agreement," Scott explained.

"Scott, let me say this. This is quite an accomplishment. You should be proud of yourself. I want you to know that your company appreciates what you have done. Not only did you save an account, you helped the company create a satisfied customer that we can use as a reference. That is a lot. I want to say thank you." John held out his hand to congratulate Scott and gave him a few warm pats on his back.

"I am happy that our client is happy. It is my job to make that happen. Thanks." Scott was a little embarrassed, but said his last words with a strong sense of satisfaction.

About the Authors

Ho-Wing Sit is the author of *Lateral Approach to Creating Success: Simple Principles for Not Leaving Success to Chance Whether You Manage a Small Shop or a Million Dollar Corporation*, *Lateral Approach to Managing Projects: Simple Principles for Achieving High Customer Satisfaction and Mutual Profitability*, and *Lateral Approach to Taking Charge: Simple Principles for New Bosses on Building Authority and Partnerships*.

Mr. Sit has been pursuing, refining, and applying powerful and effective management principles and techniques for over 30 years. In this latest work, *The Lateral Approach to Managing Projects*, he discloses the three keys to creating happy customers and successful projects, and offers easy exercises for putting them into everyday practice.

Also an inventor, Mr. Sit has been awarded four patents covering a wide range of technical subject matter. He enjoys creative painting and Ikebana, Japanese floral arrangements. Mr. Sit holds a Bachelor of Science degree in mechanical engineering and a Master of Science degree in electrical engineering from the Illinois Institute of Technology, and a Master of Business Administration degree from the Massachusetts Institute of Technology..

Ling Bundgaard is the co-author of *Lateral Approach to Creating Success: Simple Principles for Not Leaving Success to Chance Whether You Manage a Small Shop or a Million Dollar Corporation*, *Lateral Approach to Managing Projects: Simple Principles for Achieving High Customer Satisfaction and Mutual Profitability*, and *Lateral Approach to Taking Charge: Simple Principles for New Bosses on Building Authority and Partnerships*.

During her 31-year tenure at Intel Corporation, Ms. Bundgaard managed many large projects. As General Manager, she started up the first manufacturing plant in Shanghai, China, establishing the first major corporate commitment from Intel inside China. Ms Bundgaard also managed several large cross-cultural projects in other countries including the Philippines and Denmark.

Ms. Bundgaard excels at bringing people and information together to solve problems. She has found that people embrace the basic principles in the Lateral Approach book series once they understand how they stand to benefit from these principles. She believes in lifelong learning and enthusiastically shares in her writing her most memorable nuggets from peers, bosses, and mystics in business.